Jean Vanier

Becoming Human

Jean Vanier

Jean Vanier is the son of former governor general of Canada George Vanier, and founder of L'Arche, an international network of communities for people with developmental disabilities.

In 1964, after years of studying and teaching philosophy and theology, Vanier bought a house in Trosly-Breuil, France, and invited two men with developmental disabilities to live with him. He named the home L'Arche, after Noah's ark — both a place of refuge and of new beginnings.

L'Arche is now a network of more than one hundred communities in thirty countries, inhabited by people with disabilities and their caregivers. Their goal is to achieve a sense of community and dignity not possible within an institution.

He is also co-founder, with Marie-Hélène Mathieu, of Faith and Light, which brings together people with disabilities, their parents and friends, for regular times of meeting. There are now 1,300 Faith and Light communities in seventy-five countries.

Vanier has written many books, including *Finding Peace*, *Made for Happiness*, *Encountering the Other*, and *Befriending the Stranger*.

This edition published in 2008 in association with
House of Anansi Press Inc.
110 Spadina Ave., Suite 801
Toronto, ON, M5V 2K4

Library of Congress Control Number: 2008928184

ISBN: 978-0-8091-4587-4

Published by Paulist Press
997 Macarthur Boulevard
Mahwah, New Jersey 07430

Printed and bound in Canada

MIX
Paper from
responsible sources
FSC® C004071
FSC
www.fsc.org

ANCIENT FOREST ™
FRIENDLY

Contents

INTRODUCTION

LIKE ALL OF US, I have my story. Mine began as a young person of thirteen when I journeyed from Canada to England and joined the Royal Naval College in 1942. It was the middle of the war with Nazi Germany, and I had decided to prepare myself to serve on warships. I spent eight years in the navy. I left the navy in 1950 searching for another road to peace. I went to live in a small Christian community near Paris. We worked manually, we pursued studies in philosophy and theology, and we prayed together.

Then in April 1964 I went to visit a holy priest — a man of God. He was chaplain to a small institution for people with intellectual disabilities. It was there I discovered the plight of men and women who had been put aside, looked down upon, sometimes laughed at or scorned. They were seen as misfits of nature, not as human beings.

Touched and hurt by the way so many were treated, I was able to buy a little house in a village north of Paris and to welcome two men with disabilities from a sad and violent institution. Philippe Seux and Raphael Simi had each had a viral disease when they were children. The result of their illnesses had left them with significant disabilities. They never went to school, and when their parents died they were put into this dismal asylum.

And so the first community of L'Arche was born. Today, forty-four years later, there are 134 such communities in thirty-five different countries. In these communities men and women with disabilities can develop in a spirit of freedom. We live together — those with disabilities and those who wish to have a deep and sometimes lasting relationship with them. We laugh and cry and sometimes fight with one another; we work, we celebrate life, and we pray together.

Believe it or not, it has been this life together that has helped me become more human. Those I have lived with have helped me to recognize and accept my own weaknesses and vulnerability. I no longer have to pretend I am strong or clever or better than others. I am like everybody else, with my fragilities and my gifts.

Becoming Human may seem a strange title. Aren't we already human? How can we become what we already are? Like all animals, we are conceived, we are born, we grow, we give birth to others like us, and we die. What then is different?

We humans are conscious of our growth from the nakedness of birth to the nakedness of death, and we are conscious of the freedom we have to orientate our lives in one direction or another. This freedom can lead us into anguish and a fear of becoming, or it can lead us into growth and new life.

So human beings are in continual evolution. Every generation wants to achieve more than the preceding one. We are in a culture of competition. The strong, the beautiful, the intelligent, and the capable are magnified and extolled. The weak and the vulnerable are often put aside. Our world is characterized by the huge gap between the rich and the poor, the oppressors and the oppressed, and by continual horrible conflicts between national, ethnic, and religious groups.

This struggle, which has existed in various forms throughout history, is in me and in each one of us. But history has also seen women and men rise up, seeking new ways of creating peace and unity amongst people and helping the oppressed to find new life through wisdom and love and a consciousness of their value.

So to become human implies two realities. It means to be someone, to have cultivated our gifts, and also to be open to others, to look at them not with a feeling of superiority but with eyes of respect. It means to become men and women with the wisdom of love. For this, we often need help. For many, as for myself, religion can be a gentle source of strength and love, as can a mentor or wise friend.

We cannot know what crises await humanity because of

the way we have treated our earth, because of our greed and our lack of respect for life or for others, because of the immense inequalities in living standards and opportunities between people, or because of world conflicts and the misuse of power.

But the future of humanity is not just in the hands of politicians and of corporations but in our hands. Peace will come through dialogue, through trust and respect for others who are different, through inner strength and a spirituality of love, patience, humility, and forgiveness. Little by little, a culture of competition will be transformed into a culture of welcome and mutual respect. The crises that will come will then not just be moments of danger but opportunities for dialogue and unity, and solutions will emerge.

I am on the eve of my departure, but young people are just entering into this adventure of becoming. This new generation is searching for ways to live a new vision. They are finding inspiration in Mahatma Gandhi, Martin Luther King, Nelson Mandela, Mother Theresa, Etty Hillesum, and so many others. My hope is that more and more of us will seek this road of peacemaking by living in the reality of mutual acceptance, building places of belonging where each one is helped to grow in freedom from fear and the different forms of egoism that can drive us apart, and where we can all learn to celebrate in forgiveness.

Jean Vanier
Trosly-Breuil, France
March 2008

I

LONELINESS

THIS BOOK IS ABOUT the liberation of the human heart from the tentacles of chaos and loneliness, and from those fears that provoke us to exclude and reject others. It is a liberation that opens us up and leads us to the discovery of our common humanity. I want to show that this discovery is a journey from loneliness to a love that transforms, a love that grows in and through belonging, a belonging that can include as well as exclude. The discovery of our common humanity liberates us from self-centred compulsions and inner hurts; it is the discovery that ultimately finds its fulfillment in forgiveness and in loving those who are our enemies. It is the process of truly becoming human.

This book is not essentially about the formation and organization of society; it is not essentially political in scope. But since society is made up of individuals, as we open up to others and allow ourselves to be concerned with their condition, then the society in which we live must also change and become more open. We will begin to work together for the common good. On the other hand, if we commit ourselves to the making of a society in which we are concerned only with our own rights, then that society must become more and more closed in on itself. Where we do not feel any responsibility towards others, there is no reason for us to work harmoniously towards the common good.

Over the last thirty-four years, my experience has been primarily with men and women who have intellectual disabilities. In August 1964, I founded l'Arche: a network of small homes and communities where we live together, men and women with intellectual disabilities and those who feel called to share their lives with them. Today, there are over one hundred l'Arche communities in the world. Living in l'Arche, I have discovered a lot about loneliness, belonging, and the inner pain that springs from a sense of rejection. Community life with men and women who have intellectual disabilities has taught me a great deal about what it means to be human. To some, it may sound strange for me to say that it is the weak, and those who have been excluded from society, who have been my teachers. I hope that I can reveal a bit of what I have learned — and am still learning — about being human, and about helping others to discover our common humanity.

It was only in l'Arche that I really discovered what loneliness is. There were probably many times before l'Arche when I had felt lonely but until then I had not seen loneliness as a painful reality, maybe because I had succeeded in keeping myself busy by doing things. Perhaps I had never named it or needed to give it a name.

When I started welcoming those with intellectual disabilities into l'Arche, men and women from institutions, psychiatric hospitals, dysfunctional families, I began to realize how lonely they were. I discovered the terrible feeling of chaos that comes from extreme loneliness.

A sense of loneliness can be covered up by the things we do as we seek recognition and success. This is surely what I did as a young adult. It is what we all do. We all have this drive to do things that will be seen by others as valuable, things that make us feel good about ourselves and give us a sense of being alive. We only become aware of loneliness at times when we cannot perform or when imagination seems to fail us.

Loneliness can appear as a faint dis-ease, an inner dissatisfaction, a restlessness in the heart.

Loneliness comes at any time. It comes in times of sickness or when friends are absent; it comes during sleepless nights when the heart is heavy, during times of failure at work or in relationships; it comes when we lose trust in ourselves and in others. In old age, loneliness can rise up and threaten to overwhelm us. At such times, life can lose its meaning. Loneliness can feel like death.

When people are physically well, performing creatively, successful in their lives, loneliness seems absent. But I believe that loneliness is something essential to human nature; it can only be covered over, it can never actually go away. Loneliness is part of being human, because there is nothing in existence that can completely fulfill the needs of the human heart.

Loneliness in one form is, in fact, essential to our

humanity. Loneliness can become a source of creative energy, the energy that drives us down new paths to create new things or to seek more truth and justice in the world. Artists, poets, mystics, prophets, those who do not seem to fit into the world or the ways of society, are frequently lonely. They feel themselves to be different, dissatisfied with the status quo and with mediocrity; dissatisfied with our competitive world where so much energy goes into ephemeral things. Frequently, it is the lonely man or woman who revolts against injustice and seeks new ways. It is as if a fire is burning within them, a fire fuelled by loneliness.

Loneliness is the fundamental force that urges mystics to a deeper union with God. For such people, loneliness has become intolerable but, instead of slipping into apathy or anger, they use the energy of loneliness to seek God. It pushes them towards the absolute. An experience of God quenches this thirst for the absolute but at the same time, paradoxically, whets it, because this is an experience that can never be total; by necessity, the knowledge of God is always partial. So loneliness opens up mystics to a desire to love each and every human being as God loves them.

Loneliness, then, can be a force for good. More frequently, however, loneliness shows other, less positive faces. It can be a source of apathy and depression, and even of a desire to die. It can push us into escapes and addictions in the need to forget our inner pain and emptiness. This apathy is how loneliness most often shows itself in the elderly and in those with disabilities.

It is the loneliness we find in those who fall into depression, who have lost the sense of meaning in their lives, who are asking the question born of despair: What is left?

I once visited a psychiatric hospital that was a kind of warehouse of human misery. Hundreds of children with severe disabilities were lying, neglected, on their cots. There was a deadly silence. Not one of them was crying. When they realize that nobody cares, that nobody will answer them, children no longer cry. It takes too much energy. We cry out only when there is hope that someone may hear us.

Such loneliness is born of the most complete and utter depression, from the bottom of the deepest pit in which the human soul can find itself. The loneliness that engenders depression manifests itself as chaos. There is confusion, and coming out of this confusion there can be a desire for self-destruction, for death. So, loneliness can become agony, a scream of pain. There is no light, no consolation, no touch of peace and of the joy life brings. Such loneliness reveals the true meaning of chaos.

Life no longer flows in recognizable patterns. For the person engulfed in this form of loneliness there is only emptiness, anguish, and inner agitation; there are no yearnings, no desires to be fulfilled, no desire to live. Such a person feels completely cut off from everyone and everything. It is a life turned in upon itself. All order is gone and those in this chaos are unable to relate or listen to others. Their lives seem to have no meaning. They live in complete confusion, closed up in themselves.

Thus loneliness can become such uncontrolled anguish that one can easily slip into the chaos of madness.

Let me tell you some stories, from my own experience, of the damage loneliness can create. I met Eric for the first time in 1977. He was in the children's ward of the local psychiatric hospital, 40 kilometres from the l'Arche community in Trosly, France. He was blind and deaf, as well as severely intellectually disabled; he could neither walk nor eat by himself. He came to l'Arche at the age of sixteen, full of tremendous needs, anguish, and fears. He often sat on the ground and whenever he felt someone close by, would stretch out his arms and try to clutch that person and to climb up on them. Once he had succeeded in getting someone to hold him, his actions would become wild: he would lose control, struggling to be held and, at the same time, jumping up and down. Holding Eric under these conditions became intolerable for anyone and, inevitably, it ended in a struggle, trying to get rid of him as he fought to remain held. He was someone who seemed to be living in immense anguish.

Anguish is inner agitation, a chaotic, unfocused energy. Anguish breaks sleep and other patterns and brings us to a place of confusion. To be lonely is to feel unwanted and unloved, and therefore unloveable. Loneliness is a taste of death. No wonder some people who are desperately lonely lose themselves in mental illness or violence to forget the inner pain.

Eric was a terribly lonely young man. He needed to be loved but his needs were so great that no one person could fulfill them. It took a long time in l'Arche before he found some inner peace. Little by little, as he learned to trust those around him, he discovered he was loved.

By way of contrast, Pierre was the seventh child in a family of thirteen, a man who had spent seven years in prison. I met him in Montreal. He had run away from home when he was twelve years old because he felt unnoticed and unwanted by his family. So, for a long time he lived with gangs on the street. In his heart, Pierre was a lonely man who felt lost. He had nowhere to go, no meaning in his life. He needed a friend, a teacher, someone who could help him find himself and a sense of purpose.

When he was sixteen Pierre committed a crime, which I believe was a cry for help. He went to jail for it. While he was there, he fell in love with a woman who regularly visited the prison. They got married and his life took on new meaning; he finally had someone and something to live for. It was the beginning of his process of becoming human, and it happened because he felt loved.

In our l'Arche communities we experience that deep inner healing comes about mainly when people feel loved, when they have a sense of belonging. Our communities are essentially places where people can serve and create, and, most importantly, where they can love as well as be loved. This healing flows from relationships — it is not something automatic.

I have come to learn that embodied in this approach there is an important principle: the necessity of human commitment to the evolution of the new, the necessity of accepting constant movement as the key to our humanity and as the only road to becoming truly human.

In Eric and Pierre, there were chaos and disorder. Yet in the midst of the chaos there was a way out. Are not all our lives a movement from order to disorder, which in turn evolves into a new order?

Order and Disorder

The passage of life itself suggests a constantly recurring pattern of movement from order to chaos, from chaos to order, again and again.

Birth, adolescence, and old age are all passages that are filled with anguish. Finally there is the ultimate corruption and disorder that death brings. Throughout our lives there is the disorder created by sickness, accidents, loss of work, loss of friends — all the crises that destroy our agendas, security, and carefully laid plans. Such disorder demands a gradual re-ordering of our lives and the period of transition such a crisis represents is not an easy one to live through. It is a time of loss, when we have yet to receive something new. It is a time of grief.

In human beings, there is a constant tension between order and disorder, connectedness and loneliness, evolution and revolution, security and insecurity. Our universe is constantly evolving: the old order gives way to a new order and this in its turn crumbles when the next order appears. It is no different in our lives in the movement from birth to death.

Change of one sort or another is the essence of life, so there will always be the loneliness and insecurity that come with change. When we refuse to accept that loneliness and insecurity are part of life, when we refuse to accept that they are the price of change, we close the door on many possibilities for ourselves; our lives become lessened, we are less than fully human. If we try to prevent, or ignore, the movement of life, we run the risk of falling into the inevitable depression that must accompany an impossible goal. Life evolves; change is constant. When we try to prevent the forward movement of life, we may succeed for a while but, inevitably, there is an explosion; the groundswell of life's constant movement, constant change, is too great to resist.

And so empires of ideas, as well as empires of wealth and power, come and go. To live well is to observe in today's apparent order the tiny anomalies that are the seeds of change, the harbingers of the order of tomorrow. This means living in a state of a certain insecurity, in anguish and loneliness, which, at its best, can push us towards the new. Too much security and the refusal to evolve, to embrace change, leads to a kind of death. Too much insecurity, however, can also mean death. To be human is to create sufficient order so that we can move on into insecurity and seeming disorder. In this way, we discover the new.

Those who have the eyes to see this new order, as it arises, will often be considered too revolutionary, too modern, too liberal. Dictators everywhere have clamped down on movements for liberation; those who lead are always so certain that anarchy will arise if they do not govern with a firm hand. In reality, leaders are frightened of sharing or losing power. They too are frightened of change. They want to control everything. Those who see the coming new order will frequently be alone, persecuted.

But how do we learn to read the signs of evolution and to see where it is going? We can only help the new to evolve if we have certain clear principles. Here are five principles that have helped me.

First: all humans are sacred, whatever their culture, race, or religion, whatever their capacities or incapacities, and whatever their weaknesses or strengths may be. Each of us has an instrument to bring to the vast orchestra of humanity, and each of us needs help to become all that we might be.

Second: our world and our individual lives are in the process of evolving. Evolution is a part of life but it is not always easy to determine the good and the bad in something that is evolving. How to maintain the old and prepare the way for the new? It is not a question of rejecting the past but of letting the past flow into the present and letting this process guide us as to how to live in the future. It is a question of loving all the essential values of the past and reflecting on how they are to be lived in the new. These values include openness, love, wholeness, unity, peace, the human potential for healing and redemption, and, most important, the necessity of forgiveness. So, everything that permits and encourages the flow of life and growth is necessary.

Third: maturity comes through working with others, through dialogue, and through a sense of belonging and a searching together. In order to evolve towards greater maturity and wholeness, we humans need a certain security; only when we have attained this can we advance in insecurity with others towards the new.

Fourth: human beings need to be encouraged to make choices, and to become responsible for their own lives and for the lives of others. We need to be encouraged to evolve in order to become mature, and to break out of the shell of self-centredness and out of our defence mechanisms, which are as oppressive to others as they are to ourselves. In other words, we humans need to be rooted in good earth in order to produce good fruit. But for this we need to freely risk life in order to give of ourselves.

Fifth: in order to make such choices, we need to reflect and to seek truth and meaning. Reality is the first principle of truth. To be human means to remain connected to our humanness and to reality. It means to abandon the loneliness of being closed up in illusions, dreams, and ideologies, frightened of reality, and to choose to move towards connectedness. To be human is to accept ourselves just as we are, with our own history, and to accept others as they are. To be human means to accept history as it is and to work, without fear, towards greater openness, greater understanding, and a greater love of others. To be human is not to be crushed by reality, or to be angry about it or to try to hammer it into what we think it is or should be, but to commit ourselves as individuals, and as a species, to an evolution that will be for the good of all.

Each one of us needs to work at searching for truth, not be afraid of it. We need to strive to live in truth, because the truth sets us free, even if it means living in loneliness and anguish at certain moments. Perhaps this search for truth is a process of letting ourselves be enfolded in truth rather than possessing truth, as if it were an object that we could possess, that we could use against others.

The truth will set us free only if we let it penetrate our hearts and rend the veil that separates head from heart. It is important not only to join the head and the heart, but to love truth, also, and to let it inspire our lives, our attitudes, and our way of living. The truth of religion and morality shows itself when they liberate us and give us a deep respect and compassion for others.

This process of searching for truth demands an openness; it demands an evolution of thought, for individuals and entire societies, as the whole world changes and we discover new intimations of what *is*. There are unchanging principles, such as the call to be people of love and not of hate, which govern our lives. We need to integrate our experiences into these principles and let these principles enlighten our experience.

Such an evolution in thought can mean searching and groping in the dark, sometimes in anguish, thinking through old ideas, formulating them in new words and new ways. Philosophy, anthropology, theology, and those sciences that tell us what it means to be human can be dangerous if they become ideologies that dictate reality; instead, they need to be understood as the means by which we humbly listen to and marvel at reality.

We must not try to return to the past, but instead launch out into the future — to understand each other and what it means to be human, to understand what is happening in the world — in order to become more fully human and to work for peace and unity. It is only as we begin to integrate such a sense of reality more fully into our being, as we thirst for that which gives meaning to our lives, that we discover the fundamental meaning of loneliness: a cry, often a painful cry of anguish, for more respect and love of others, to be even more enfolded in truth, held in God. Such a cry could bring a new wholeness to humanity.

Community and Rigid Order

The continual search for meaning and order and for an antidote to loneliness leads us to the necessity of community.

There are some families, tribes, and groups that are beautifully ordered, where the imposed order seems to be a successful solution to the chaos of life, where each person feels safe because they are connected to the others. This seeming order and safety, however, can be dangerous; in such a community, individuals can be stifled, prevented from evolving.

Everytime I go to Africa, I am struck by how different African cultures are from our Western culture. The main difference is the sense of community. If the image of Western society is that of the hustling, bustling city populated by competing individuals, then the contrasting image of African societies is that of the village, the embodiment of community.

In the villages of African countries I have visited, people are rarely lonely. To begin with, they live very close together. Children often sleep together, in the same room. Courtyards are filled with aunts, uncles, cousins, and relatives of every sort. All are bonded together under the often strict and powerful guidance of a chief or group of elders.

In such a milieu, everyone tends to toe the line. There is little place for individuality or creative initiative; senior members of the community even take over such personal functions as finding work and arranging marriages. Belonging, in such a context, gives each member of the family a sense of security.

There can be something beautifully human in such villages; men have their roles, the women theirs. However, the price paid for such order and security is the great difficulty individuals have in freeing themselves from the power of the group, to liberate their true, deepest self, to search for the new.

This touches on a real paradox: as humans, we crave belonging, we need the connectedness to others that brings security, but this connectedness can prevent the natural movement and evolution that we need in our lives. It can also get in the way of creativity and stifle the natural loneliness that pushes us to discover something new, that pushes us closer to God. This loneliness is the loneliness of the individual who steps out from the group, who takes a chance on what can be discovered and done outside of the norm.

So here is the paradox: as humans we are caught between competing drives, the drive to belong, to fit in and be a part of something bigger than ourselves, and the drive to let our deepest selves rise up, to walk alone, to refuse the accepted and the comfortable, and this can mean, at least for a time, the acceptance of anguish. It is in the group that we discover what we have in common. It is as individuals that we discover a personal relationship

with God. We must find a way to balance our two oppos-
ing impulses.

The Weakness of a Child

Where do these competing drives, the need to be fully
oneself and the need for community, come from?

We were all conceived and born in littleness and weakness. We could do nothing by ourselves. We depended
totally on our parents for food and for protection; our
greatest need was for their enfolding, protective, and
stimulating love. Children cannot live and grow humanly
without that love. For a human being, love is as vital as food.

When children are loved, they live off trust; their bodies
and hearts open up to those who respect and love them, who
understand and listen to them. They begin to blossom.

What happens when a child feels unloved, unwanted?
There is nothing to compare with the terrible loneliness of
a child; fragile and helpless, a lonely child feels fear,
anguish, a sense of guilt. And when children are wounded
in their hearts, they learn to protect themselves by hiding
behind barriers.

Lonely children feel no commonality with adults. They
have lost trust in them and in themselves, they are confused and feel misunderstood. Lonely children cannot
name the pain. Only self-accusation remains.

However, life wants to live. If some children fall into
depression and want to die, others seem to survive des-
pite adverse conditions such as sickness, squalor, abuse,
violence, and abandonment; life can be tenacious and
stubborn. Instinctively, all children learn to hide their

terrible feelings behind inner walls, the shadowy areas of their being. All the disorder and darkness of their lives can be buried there. They then throw themselves into their lives, into the search for approbation, into self-fulfillment, into dreams and illusions.

Hurts and pain can transform into the energy that pushes children forward. Such children can then become individuals protected by the barriers they had to build around their vulnerable, wounded hearts. Children who are less wounded will have fewer barriers. They will find it easier to live in the world and to work with others; they will not be as closed in on themselves.

The lonely child is unable to connect with others. There is a lonely child in each of us, hidden behind the walls we created in order to survive. I am speaking, of course, of only one aspect of loneliness, the loneliness that can destroy some part of us, not the loneliness that creates. How might we begin to find a way to overcome the terrible legacy that destructive loneliness leaves us? I can only speak from my own experience, so let me tell you about Claudia.

Love Transforms Chaos

In 1975, we welcomed Claudia into our l'Arche community in Suyapa, a slum area of Tegucigalpa, Honduras. She was seven years old and had spent practically her whole life in a dismal, overcrowded asylum. Claudia was blind, fearful of relationships, filled with inner pain and anguish. Technically speaking she was autistic.

Her anguish seemed to increase terribly when she

arrived in the community, probably because in leaving the asylum, she lost her reference points, as well as the structured existence that had given her a certain security. Everything and everyone frightened her; she screamed day and night and smeared excrement on the walls. She seemed totally mad; overwhelmed by insecurity, her personality appeared to be disintegrating.

Claudia lived a horrible form of madness which should not be idealized or seen as a gateway to another world. In l'Arche, we have learned from our own experience of healing, as well as through the help of psychiatrists and psychologists, that chaos, or "madness," has meaning; it comes from somewhere, it is comprehensible. Madness is an immense cry, a sickness. It is a way of escaping when the stress of being in a world of pain is too great. Madness is an escape from anguish. But there is an order in the disorder that can permit healing, if only it can be found.

Twenty years after she first arrived at Suyapa, I visited the community and met Claudia again; I found her quite well. She was by then a twenty-eight-year-old woman, still blind and autistic but at peace and able to do many things in the community. She still liked being alone but she was clearly not a lonely person. She would often sing to herself and there was a constant smile on her face.

She did get angry at times, when she felt she was not being respected or was put in a situation that provoked feelings of insecurity. One day, I was sitting opposite to her at lunch and said, "Claudia, can I ask you a question?" She replied, "Si, Juan." "Claudia, why are you so happy?" Her answer was simple and direct: "Dios." God. I asked the community leader, Nadine, what the answer meant. Nadine said, "That is Claudia's secret."

It was loneliness and insecurity that had brought Claudia to the chaos of madness. It was community, love, and friendship that finally brought her inner peace. This movement from chaos to inner peace, from self-hate to self-trust, began when Claudia realized that she was loved.

There are, for me, seven aspects of love that seem necessary for the transformation of the heart in those who are profoundly lonely. They are: to reveal, to understand, to communicate, to celebrate, to empower, to be in communion with another, and, finally, to forgive.

To Reveal

The first aspect of love, the key aspect, is revelation. Just as a mother and father reveal to their children that they have value and beauty, so, too, did the therapist and the others who lived with Claudia reveal to Claudia her value and beauty. To reveal someone's beauty is to reveal their value by giving them time, attention, and tenderness. To love is not just to do something for them but to reveal to them their own uniqueness, to tell them that they are special and worthy of attention. We can express this revelation through our open and gentle presence, in the way we look at and listen to a person, the way we speak to and care for someone. Gestures can be filled with a respect that reveals to someone their worth, even if that worth is hidden under anger, hatred, or madness.

This revelation of value, the revelation that heals, takes time. In the case of Claudia, seven childhood years of pain in an asylum, seven years of loneliness, lack of love, and feelings of worthlessness had taken their toll. Claudia had developed survival tactics and habits founded upon her belief in her own unworthiness. Her madness and screaming were reasonable responses to a world in which nobody wanted her. It took time for the transformation, from a hatred of herself to a trust in herself, to take place.

It is easy to trust in the beauty of a little child, but how to trust in the hidden beauty of Claudia when she appeared so "mad"? That is the fundamental question; how to trust that she has a heart and that she can, little by little, receive love, be transformed by love, and then give love.

The belief in the inner beauty of each and every human being is at the heart of l'Arche, at the heart of all true education and at the heart of being human. As soon as we start selecting and judging people instead of welcoming them as they are — with their sometimes hidden beauty, as well as their more frequently visible weaknesses — we are reducing life, not fostering it. When we reveal to people our belief in them, their hidden beauty rises to the surface where it may be more clearly seen by all.

To Understand

To love also means to understand and this is the second aspect of love. Claudia needed to be understood. If no one understood her how could they help her to find inner peace and growth? Her screams were not only a sign of her inner brokenness, darkness, and anguish but also a cry for help. Difficult as it is for us to accept and come to terms with this idea, I believe that every act of violence is also a message that needs to be understood. Violence should not be answered just by greater violence but by real understanding. We must ask: where is the violence coming from? What is its meaning?

Let us go back to Claudia again.

Nadine, the community leader in Suyapa, needed help from the psychiatrist and the psychologist in caring for Claudia. In this case, she found out that Claudia needed the security of a structured day. Claudia began to learn how the day at Suyapa would evolve and how she should respond in each situation. She began to discover order and learned what to expect, as well as what was expected of her. What was important was the creation of a trusting relationship based on an understanding of Claudia's needs.

Children like Claudia, children who flee from relationships into a world of their own and who are unable to communicate verbally, need to be understood in a special way. It takes time and a great deal of attention, as well as wisdom and help from professionals, in order to learn how to interpret their cries and their body language which reveal the desires and needs they cannot name.

To Communicate

The third aspect of love is then communication. Communication is at the heart of love. Just as we need to be understood, we also need to understand ourselves and for that we usually need to be helped. Children who are quite disturbed need to have someone help them name where their disturbance is coming from. When nothing is named, confusion grows and with it comes anguish.

To name something is to bring it out of chaos, out of confusion, and to render it understandable. It is a terrible thing when certain realities, such as death, are never talked about and remain hidden. When these realities are not named, they haunt us. For example, for people of my grandmother's generation, it was forbidden to speak of sex, so sex, because it was unnamed, became powerful and controlling.

Children can then quickly discover that there is such a thing called truth; that they are not living in a chaotic world that is hypocritical, filled with only lies and pretense. Parents who admit to their children that they have been unjustly angry and ask for forgiveness are naming something: they are admitting that they are not perfect. Words and life can come together: the word can indeed become flesh.

I have learned that the process of teaching and learning, of communication, involves movement, back and forth: the one who is healed and the one who is healing constantly change places. As we begin to understand ourselves, we begin to understand others. It is part of the process of moving from idealism to reality, from the sky to the earth. We do not have to be perfect or to deny our emotions.

And here, for me, is another profound truth: understanding, as well as truth, comes not only from the intellect but also from the body. When we begin to listen to our bodies, we begin to listen to reality through our own experiences; we begin to trust our intuition, our hearts. The truth is also in the "earth" of our own bodies. So it is a question of moving from theories we have learned to listening to the reality that is in and around us. Truth flows from the earth. This is not to deny the truth that flows from teachers, from books, from tradition, from our ancestors, and from religious faith. But the two must come together. Truth from the sky must be confirmed and strengthened by truth from the earth. We must learn to listen and then to communicate.

To Celebrate

The fourth aspect of love is celebration. It is not enough to reveal to people their value, to understand and care for them. To love people is also to celebrate them. So often the Claudias of the world are seen only as problems needing to be attended to by professionals. The Claudias also need laughter and play, they need people who will celebrate life with them and manifest their joy of being with them. It was this joy and the gentle presence of Nadine and the others in Suyapa that gradually weakened Claudia's great walls of defence. Little by little, she began to trust that she was not bad, but capable of loving and being loved.

So many people with disabilities are seen by their parents and families only as a tragedy. They are surrounded by sad faces, sometimes full of pity, sometimes tears. But every child, every person, needs to know that they are a source of joy; every child, every person, needs to be celebrated. Only when all of our weaknesses are accepted as part of our humanity can our negative, broken self-images be transformed.

To Empower

The fifth aspect of love is empowerment. It is not just a question of doing things for others but of helping them to do things for themselves, helping them to discover the meaning of their lives. To love means to empower. Claudia had to learn gradually that she was responsible for her own body, for her own life, that she had authority over her actions, and that she could make choices, however small. But with this sense of responsibility for herself also came the necessity of learning to respect others. Empowerment meant that Claudia had to learn how to observe the structures of the community and make efforts to respect and love others.

Many assistants come to our l'Arche communities to help and to live with men and women who have intellectual disabilities. An assistant's role is like that of a midwife: to bring forth and help foster life, to let it develop and grow according to its own natural rhythm. Assistants in l'Arche are not there to make people with disabilities somehow "normal," but to help them to grow towards maturity. For each person in l'Arche this growth towards maturity will be different. Nadine's role, as well as the role of the other assistant, was not to control, possess, or program Claudia, but to help her blossom forth into freedom, to encourage her to grow and to accept herself as she is. Claudia's life is her own secret.

Claudia could only begin to grow as she became more conscious of the mutual belonging and mutual dependence that is at the heart of the Suyapa community, itself a mirror of the larger world. And so it was that Claudia gradually began to discover that while Nadine was calling forth new life in her, Claudia was also calling forth new life in Nadine.

We have discovered how love flows into communion, the sixth aspect of love.

To Be in Communion

Communion is mutual trust, mutual belonging; it is the to-and-fro movement of love between two people where each one gives and each one receives. Communion is not a fixed state, it is an ever-growing and deepening reality that can turn sour if one person tries to possess the other, thus preventing growth. Communion is mutual vulnerability and openness one to the other. It is liberation for both, indeed, where both are allowed to be themselves, where both are called to grow in greater freedom and openness to others and to the universe.

Trust is a beautiful form of love. When we are generous, we give money, time, knowledge. In trust, we give ourselves. But we can only give of ourselves if we trust that we will be well-received by someone. At what moment is trust born? There was a secret moment, known only to Claudia, when she recognized that she was loved.

With that realization, Claudia entered into a relationship of belonging. The opening of Claudia's heart brought about a new opening in Nadine's heart, bringing her out of her own loneliness. That moment was the birth of communion between them.

Communion is at the heart of the mystery of our humanity. It means accepting the presence of another inside oneself, as well as accepting the reciprocal call to enter into another. Communion, which implies the security and insecurity of trust, is a constant struggle against all the powers of fear and selfishness in us, as well as the seemingly resilient human need to control another person.

To a certain extent we lose control in our own lives when we are open to others. Communion of hearts is a beautiful but also a dangerous thing. Beautiful because it is a new form of liberation; it brings a new joy because we are no longer alone. We are close even if we are far away. Dangerous because letting down our inner barriers means that we can be easily hurt. Communion makes us vulnerable.

God is present in this liberating communion. That is why in the Bible John the Evangelist writes in his first letter:

> Beloved, let us love one another
> because love is from God
> and whoever loves
> is born of God and knows God   (1 John 4:7)

To Forgive

There is a seventh and final aspect of love, the most crucial of all in our equation, and that is forgiveness.

In order for Claudia to begin her journey out of chaos, she needed an experience of unconditional love. But no human being can respond fully to that need. Sometimes fatigue or any one of a number of things could make the assistants respond with irritation or anger towards

Claudia. This would wound her fragile heart. The bonding between people in communion implies that we forgive each other and that we ask each other for forgiveness.

All of us carry within ourselves brokenness, as well as shadow areas, dark corners of the spirit where uncomfortable things are hidden. Human beings cannot be constantly attentive, loving, and nonviolent. If this is true in the greater world, it is even more true in the smaller world of l'Arche, where the assistants, those who are called to share their lives with the disabled, are not, generally speaking, trained professionals who come to work for a few hours a day; on the contrary, the commitment of the assistants becomes a permanent bond that we call a "covenant relationship." As we live and work and pray together, we build a new form of family.

During her time in the community, particularly in the early days, Claudia had fits of anger. There were times when she refused any relationship or structure; she let herself be governed by her inner pain; she closed herself up within her own needs and desires. At times like that she needed to be confronted by a firm, unflinching person who would not let her escape into anguish, loneliness, or folly. But Claudia could accept this only if she knew that she was respected and that she could turn to that person for help and protection. Authority that is not based on this fundamental trust, the assent of those who are led, can only be oppressive, destructive of personal freedom. Only an authority based on trust can permit growth to inner peace and freedom.

In order for Claudia to grow peacefully towards

womanhood, she needed to gradually accept not only her physical blindness but also her inner depression and anger, the scars, even open wounds, that flowed from her experience of rejection and lack of love and under-standing during the years in the asylum. It was important that Claudia discover her shadow areas, even if she could not name them, and that she learn that it was acceptable to be less than perfect. It was for Nadine to show Claudia that we are all subject to a higher, more profound law, one that we do not make but which is given to us, hidden in the heart of every human being, to reveal that life is all about growth and that it is possible for each one of us to evolve out of darkness and chaos into light and into a new order of love.

Claudia's growth was subject then to Nadine's growth. How could Nadine accept Claudia in all her chaos or madness if Nadine refused to accept the chaotic aspects and shadow areas in her own life? How could she trust in Claudia's growth if she did not trust in her own growth?

In the case of Claudia, there was a place where much of this spiritual struggle and growth occured: in prayer.

Praying Together

For most people, prayer necessitates stepping back from the pains and joys of daily life. We need this stepping back, particularly from all that is difficult or conflict-ridden, taking for ourselves a certain distance, in order to look at things not just from our own self-centred perspec-tive but from the perspective of the vision we are seeking together. That vision is to create a place of love and belonging. Prayer is a time to let light flow into our lives, to literally "enlighten" each day.

Our daily life in l'Arche is filled with so much. So many things to do and so little time. We need space to re-read the day, as it were. We need time to listen to the inner voice of hope calling us back to the essentials of love, essentials that we may have forgotten because of busyness and self-ishness. To pray, then, is more about listening than about talking. To pray is to be centred in love; it is to let what is deepest within us come to the surface. For me, it is all that and more. Prayer is also a meeting with the One who loves me, who reveals to me my secret value, who empowers me to give life, who loves us all, and who calls us forth to greater love and compassion. Prayer is resting in the quiet, gentle presence of God.

Every evening the community in Honduras would gather together to pray, a simple prayer of trust and of love, calling the Spirit of God to each person. Claudia entered freely and easily into this time of prayer, opening her heart to God. Before God, at prayers, Nadine, Claudia, and everyone in the community were on an equal footing. Each one could ask for forgiveness for the hardness of their heart; each could give thanks for the love and the life they experienced; each could ask for the strength to rid themselves of selfishness.

As Claudia began to trust that she was loved not only by Nadine but also by God, it became easier for her to love herself, easier for her to believe that she could grow in love and service, to God and to others, and that she too could give life to others. Thus she gradually found a meaning in her life. She, too, had come from God, a God of love, and was going to God. The journey through life becomes meaningful through love.

Loneliness seems to be an essentially human experience. It is not just about being alone. Loneliness is not the same thing as solitude. We can be alone yet happy, because we know that we are part of a family, a community, even the universe itself. Loneliness is a feeling of not being part of anything, of being cut off. It is a feeling of being unworthy, of not being able to cope in the face of a universe that seems to work against us.

Loneliness is a feeling of being guilty. Of what? Of existing? Of being judged? By whom? We do not know. Loneliness is a taste of death.

Many people engulfed in chaos today were conceived and born in chaos; they have known little else but abuse and hate. Since they have never received love, they remain unable to give love. As they were engulfed in chaos at an early age so now they can only transmit chaos. Love, like fear and hate, is communicated from generation to generation.

Does that mean that chaos is inevitable, that the world's pain and hatred are all caused by the inability of parents to give their children unconditional love? Are we all more or less predisposed to oppression and conflict and, thus, to chaos? Jean-Paul Sartre said that love is only an illusion. Was he right?

My belief and my experience have shown me that there

is a way out; it is the subject of this book. But this way out requires that we all discover our fundamental beauty as human beings — our capacity to give life and to receive it from others. So much of what I've said in this chapter is about the individual and what the individual can do. But what about the larger picture? Is there a political and social solution? What sort of society do we want?

There are for me a few principles. A society that encourages us to break open the shell of selfishness and self-centredness contains the seeds of a society where people are honest, truthful, and loving. A society can function well only if those within are concerned, not only with their own needs or the needs of those who immediately surround them, but by the needs of all, that is to say, by the common good and the family of nations. Each one of us, I believe, is on a journey towards this openness where we risk to love.

Growth towards openness means dialogue, trusting in others, listening to them, particularly to those who say things we don't like to hear, speaking together about our mutual needs and how we might grow to new things. The birth of a good society comes when people start to trust each other, to share with each other, and to feel concerned for each other.

The next chapter is about belonging: the essential need we have to be and to share with others. The human heart is a place of freedom. We can be obliged to follow the law but not to love, because "true love casts out fear." Our society grows in justice and peace as we allow energies of love and concern for all to rise up in ourselves.

I I

BELONGING

THE FIRST CHAPTER was about loneliness, the emptiness
we feel when we are isolated and all alone. The basic
human need is for at least one person who believes and
trusts in us. But that is never enough, it doesn't stop there.
Each of us needs to belong, not just to one person but to
a family, friends, a group, and a culture. So this chapter
is about belonging.

Belonging is important for our growth to independence;
even further, it is important for our growth to inner freedom and maturity. It is only through belonging that
we can break out of the shell of individualism and self-
centredness that both protects and isolates us.

However, the human drive for belonging also has its
pitfalls.

There is an innate need in our hearts to identify with a
group, both for protection and for security, to discover
and affirm our identity, and to use the group to prove our
worthiness and goodness, indeed, even to prove that we
are better than others. It is my belief that it is not religion

or culture at the root of human conflict but the way in which groups use religion or culture to dominate one another. Let me hasten to add that if it were not religion or culture that people used as a stick with which to beat others, they would just use something else.

Are human beings basically evil? The French philosopher, Jean-Paul Sartre, maintained that love is only one person's freedom eating up another's freedom. Are we all called to live and die in conflict? Do all our generous acts merely conceal the need to be superior to others?

Sartre leads me to my main point: What is the need to belong? Is it only a way of dealing with personal insecurity, sharing in the sense of identity that a group provides? Or is this sense of belonging an important part of everyone's journey to freedom? Is the sense of belonging akin to the earth itself, a nurturing medium that allows plants and trees to grow and to share their flowers and fruits with all?

A group is the manifestation of this need to belong. A group can, however, close in on itself, believing that it is superior to others. But my vision is that belonging should be at the heart of a fundamental discovery: that we all belong to a common humanity, the human race. We may be rooted in a specific family and culture but we come to this earth to open up to others, to serve them and receive the gifts they bring to us, as well as to all of humanity.

In 1986, l'Arche founded a community in Bethany, in the West Bank, just a few miles from Jerusalem. Our house was located in a Palestinian Muslim area, not far from the mosque. All our neighbours were Muslim as were the owners of our house, Ali and Fatma, who lived on the top floor and did everything they could to make us feel at ease. Marie-Antoinette and Kathy, the leaders of l'Arche, welcomed two young women, Rula and Ghadir, and a few other people with disabilities from the local area.

Whenever I visited the little community, I was touched by Ghadir's beauty. She suffered from cerebral palsy and couldn't speak, but her smile, her trust, and her shining eyes welcomed me each time I came. Through her body, she "spoke" so lovingly. I was touched also by the pain in the heart of Rula's mother. Rula lived in terrible anguish and sometimes she would scream for hours. The tears of her mother were no different from the tears of a Christian or Jewish mother.

We human beings are all fundamentally the same. We all belong to a common, broken humanity. We all have wounded, vulnerable hearts. Each one of us needs to feel appreciated and understood; we all need help. Through Rula and Ghadir, I saw more clearly how those who are weak and in need have a secret power to touch our hearts and to bring us together in mutual belonging, whatever our religion or culture.

People with intellectual disabilities are so similar, wherever you go. From their place of obvious weakness, they most often respond to love, a love that reveals to them their value, a love that understands. They radiate a certain peace and seem to attract others through their love and trust. If our little community in Bethany was accepted in the neighbourhood, it was because of Ghadir, Rula, and the others.

During my frequent visits to the community, I often
went to Jerusalem, only a few miles away. Most of the
Jewish people I met could not understand why we wanted
to live with Palestinians. "Aren't you in danger?" they
would ask. Our Palestinian friends were not happy, either,
that we had contact with Jewish people. It was difficult for
both sides to see the beauty of the person hidden under
the cloak of a different religion and a different culture.
And the reactions of our Jewish and Palestinian friends
are really no different than the reactions most of us tend
to have towards those from other groups. We judge them
according to our fears and prejudices.

I remember a weekend in Ottawa in the 1970s, when I
helped to organize a meeting with men in prison; a group
of ex-inmates and offenders, prison guards, policemen,
prison chaplains, prison directors, and psychologists.
We shared together, ate together, slept in dormitories.
Nobody carried any label or sign showing to which group
they belonged. We were together as persons, not as representatives of a group. It was, if you like, an image for me
of how we actually behave towards each other when we
have no "markers" to tell us what we are supposed to feel
towards someone. It was also a small indication of what
society might look like, and how it might function, if we
could overcome our prejudices.

The illusion of being superior engenders the need to
prove it; and so oppression is born. A bishop in Africa
told me that, even though there were few Christians in
the area, he had built his cathedral bigger than the local
mosque. All this to prove that Christianity was a better,

more powerful religion than Islam. So we build walls
around our group and cultivate our certitudes. Prejudice
grows on such walls.

How did we, the human race, get to this position where
we judge it natural not just to band ourselves into groups,
but to set ourselves group against group, neighbour
against neighbour, in order to establish some ephemeral
sense of superiority?

One of the fundamental issues for people to examine is
how to break down these walls that separate us one from
another; how to open up one to another; how to create
trust and places of dialogue.

Back to the Child

Our lives are a mystery of growth from weakness to weakness, from the weakness of the little baby to the weakness
of the aged. Throughout our lives, we are prone to fatigue,
sickness, and accidents. Weakness is at the heart of each
one of us. Weakness becomes a place of chaos and confusion if in our weakness we are not wanted; it becomes a
place of peace and joy if we are accepted, listened to,
appreciated, and loved.

Some people are infuriated by weakness; they are disturbed by the cry of a child. Weakness awakens hardness
and anger in them. Equally dangerous, if less obviously
so, weakness pushes some people to a possessive love.
However, weakness can also open up our hearts to compassion: the place where we are concerned for the growth
and well-being of the weak.

To deny weakness as a part of life is to deny death,

because weakness speaks to us of the ultimate powerlessness, of death itself. To be small, to be sick, to be dying, to be dead, are stages of powerlessness, they appear to us to be anti-life and so we deny them.

If we deny our weakness and the reality of death, if we want to be powerful and strong always, we deny a part of our being, we live an illusion. To be human is to accept who we are, this mixture of strength and weakness. To be human is to accept and love others just as they are. To be human is to be bonded together, each with our weaknesses and strengths, because we need each other. Weakness, recognized, accepted, and offered, is at the heart of belonging, so it is at the heart of communion with another.

Weakness carries within it a secret power. The cry and the trust that flow from weakness can open up hearts. The one who is weaker can call forth powers of love in the one who is stronger. Do those who are stronger respond with love because in an unconscious way they identify with the one who is weak? Do they, in some way, know that one day they too will be weak and will cry out for help, recognition, and love?

Belonging is a beautiful but terrible reality. In every relationship, there are times of light and bliss, when two people call forth that which is most beautiful in each other. They discover the joy of moving from loneliness to togetherness, of giving and receiving; each feels a certain fullness of life.

However, there are times not only of light and bliss but of darkness and depression. In each one of us, there is a shadow side, which, from time to time, manifests itself in our consciousness through anger, frustration, or depression, through the refusal to belong, because belonging appears to be something that crushes freedom. In this case, belonging can be painful.

The conception and birth of a child are a new awakening of the heart, they enlarge it. The parents are called to grow in greater love and openness, and give of themselves. The beautiful side of belonging is how it calls forth what is most precious in the human heart.

Belonging is equally beautiful for the child. She knows she is loved and that she brings joy to her parents. Her body, her growth, her nourishment, her language, and her security all come from belonging. It is through this sense of belonging that she begins to discover who she is and who she is called to become. Belonging, then, is a school of love where we learn to open up to others and to the world around us, where each person, creature, and thing in our world is important and is respected.

We do not discover who we are, we do not reach true humanness, in a solitary state; we discover it through mutual dependency, in weakness, in learning through belonging.

The Joy and Pain of Belonging

I have learned over the years how the personality and character traits of the adult are formed in the early years. As a child discovers at certain moments her parents' lack of love, their need to control or possess, and sometimes their violence and abuse, she discovers through her inner feelings of depression, anger, and revolt that belonging is a difficult, even dangerous, reality.

These moments are like a dagger in the heart, bringing the child to a place of confusion and anguish. Because she is so weak, helpless, and defenceless, she cannot possibly understand what is happening, nor can she express her anger. She has to suppress it; she pushes it down into the secret recesses of her being.

So it is that the unconscious self, the shadow area, the inner darkness in each one of us, develops. This shadow area governs and controls our future attitudes to belonging.

If children experience weakness and belonging only as a place of being crushed or manipulated instead of a place of the binding force of love, a place which allows them to be themselves, then love doesn't exist for them. It is but a mirage that eventually leads to the destruction of their personal freedom and innermost being. That is the meaning of Sartre's words when he says that love is only the eating of one person's liberty by another. Communion and trust are not, then, a sign of human plenitude but of a lack of identity, even of weakness, of an incapacity to be and to assume responsibility for one's own life. In this context, to be means to be strong, to defend oneself, to be powerful in the jungle of life. Love, vulnerability, and belonging are to be shunned.

The experience of such pain moves children, especially when they become adolescents, to forge their own identities, to own their separateness from their parents. But it can also push children into conformity and a fear of owning who they are and of expressing their pain. All the beautiful, as well as all the painful, childhood experiences affect children's development and their relationships with others and forge their character traits. Belonging is what it means to be a family. If parents have encouraged initiative and growth to freedom, if children have been listened to and helped to make their own decisions, to accept and respect others, and to be open to them, if they have been taught to live the to-and-fro of life with others, these children will later on be able to live other forms of belonging and grow to maturity with greater ease. They will be more open to others because they will have lived trust and communion of hearts.

Communion is the to-and-fro of love. It is the trust that bonds us together, children with their parents, a sick person with a nurse, a child with a teacher, a husband with a wife, friends together, people with a common task. It is the trust that comes from the intuitive knowledge that we are safe in the hands of another and that we can be open and vulnerable, one to another. Communion is not static; it is an evolving reality. Trust is continually called to grow and to deepen, or it is wounded and diminishes. It is a trust that the other will not possess or crush you but rejoices in your gifts and calls you to growth and to freedom. Such a trust calls forth trust in yourself.

One who is weak, who lives in true communion with another, will not see his own weakness as something to be judged, as something negative, he will sense that he is appreciated, that he has a place.

So, belonging can be a place of opening up as well as a place of closing in. It is the place where we discover all the things that make up our identity: family, culture, language, manhood or womanhood, how to live with our bodies, how to communicate, how to love and respect others. At the heart of belonging is the fact that we have received our existence from others and need to develop, as individuals, physically, psychologically, and humanly.

Think of the immediate society of the child as the tribe and the immediate surroundings as the village. Belonging exists not only in the family and the tribe but also, as the child goes to school, shares in village life, and discovers a wider sense of belonging with others of the same town, region, culture, religion, and language. Sometimes the child meets people in the village who are different: strangers, immigrants, people with disabilities, people from another social group or religious tradition. She will pick up quite quickly through adults' attitudes whether such people are to be accepted and loved as fellow human beings or ignored, even shunned, as those who do not belong. And so we learn that those who are different, those who are strange, are either acceptable or dangerous.

When a child acquires a language and learns how to relate to adults, to his peers, and to God, when he learns the customs and values that have been handed down through his culture, how to deal with pain, catastrophe, and death, he cannot help but think that what he has been taught is the only way of being and living. If doubt is allowed to creep in, the whole order of his life collapses. And so, at the beginning of life, we learn that there is a right way and a wrong way of doing everything. We do not question; we obey or risk courting disorder. As we grow into adolescence and adulthood, we begin to question the values learned during our childhood. That is why adolescents often go through a crisis of faith and of trust.

The Difficult Place of Those Who Are Weaker

Those who are weak have great difficulty finding their place in our society. The image of the ideal human as powerful and capable disenfranchises the old, the sick, the less-abled. For me, society must, by definition, be inclusive of the needs and gifts of all its members; how can we lay claim to making an open and friendly society where human rights are respected and fostered when, by the values we teach and foster, we systematically exclude segments of our population?

I also believe that those we most often exclude from the normal life of society, people with disabilities, have profound lessons to teach us. When we do include them, they add richly to our lives and add immensely to our world.

Our society is geared to growth, development, progress. Life, for most of us, is a race to be won. Families are about evolution: at a certain stage, children are encouraged to leave home, get married, have children of their own, move on in their lives. But people with disabilities have no such future. Once they have reached a certain level of development, they are no longer expected or encouraged to progress. There is no "promotion" for the disabled and what forward movement there is seems frequently to be either erratic or cruelly sped up: many move quite quickly from childhood to adulthood without passing through a period of adolescence; others age quickly. Our society is not set up to cope very well with people who are weaker or slower. More important, we are not skilled at listening to the wisdom of those whose life patterns are outside of the social norm.

There is a lack of synchronicity between our society and people with disabilities. A society that honours only the powerful, the clever, and the winners necessarily belittles the weak. It is as if to say: to be human is to be powerful.

Those who see the heart only as a place of weakness will be fearful of their own hearts. For them, the heart is a place of pain and anguish, of chaos and of transitory emotions. So they reject those who live essentially by their hearts, who cannot develop the same intellectual and rational capacities as others. People with intellectual disabilities are excluded; it was never intended that they be included as equal partners with the powerful, with you and me.

Our notions of society and our belief systems flow from our own fundamental experiences of life, of death, of joy, and of anguish. If we have never experienced a love that is liberating, how can we talk of love as valuable? If our journey through life has been one of conflict and power, then our image of the ideal person will be of one who prevails in conflict and wields power with assurance.

The history of our world is the history of conflicts, of one group demonstrating its strength over another. Weakness is at the heart of the need to belong; weakness that we may fear, because we have been hurt. So we band together in groups in order to share our common strength. So easily from this does conflict arise. Each group is secure in certitudes and ideology. From there it is a small step to indifference, to despisal, and to suspicion: the fear and hatred of others.

In all conflicts between groups, there are three elements. One: the certitude that our group is morally superior, possibly even chosen by God. All others should follow our example or be at our service. In order to bring peace to the world, we have to impose our set of beliefs upon others, through manipulation, force, and fear, if necessary. Two: a refusal or incapacity to see or admit to any possible errors or faults in our group. The undeniable nature of our own goodness makes us think we are infallible; there can be no wrong in us. Three: a refusal to believe that any other group possesses truth or can contribute anything of value. At best, others may be regarded as ignorant, unenlightened, and possessing only half-truths; at worst, they are seen as destructive, dangerous, and possessed by evil spirits: they need to be overpowered for the good of humanity. Society and cultures are, then, divided into the "good" and the "bad"; the good attributing to themselves the mission to save, to heal, to bring peace to a wicked world, according to their own terms and under their controlling power.

Such is the story of all civilizations through the ages as they spread over the earth by invading and colonizing. Differences must be suppressed; "savages" must be civilized. We must prove by all possible means that our culture, our power, our knowledge, and our technology are the best, that our gods are the only gods!

This is not just the story of civilizations but also of all

wars of religion, inquisitions, censorships, dictatorships; all things, in short, that are ideologies. An ideology is a set of ideas translated into a set of values. Because they are held to be absolutely true, these ideas and values need to be imposed on others if they are not readily accepted. A political system, a school of psychology, and a philosophy of economics can all be ideologies. Even a place of work can be an ideology. Religious sub-groups, sects, are based upon ideological principles. Religions themselves can become ideologies. And ideologues, by their nature, are not open to new ideas or even to debate; they refuse to accept or listen to anyone else's reality. They refuse to admit any possibility of error or even criticism of their system; they are closed up in their set of ideas, theories, and values.

We human beings have a great facility for living illusions, for protecting our self-image with power, for justifying it all by thinking we are the favoured ones of God.

And this is not only something from past history; it is our world today. The civil wars in Algeria, the genocide in Rwanda, the conflict in the former Yugoslavia, the tension between Israelis and Palestinians, the way men and women are treated in the most abominable way for their beliefs, and the way the weak, those with disabilities, are written out of the equation of life, are all signs of this need to dictate that one group is right and the other wrong.

How difficult it is for human beings to move from the recognition of the ultimate value of their own particular culture and way of life to the acceptance of the value of other cultures and ways of living. This movement implies a weakening in our own certitudes and identity, a shifting of consciousness and a lowering of protective walls. The discovery of our common humanity, beneath our differences, seems for many to be dangerous. It not only means that we have to lose some of our power, privilege, and self-image, but also that we have to look at the shadow side in ourselves, the brokenness, and even the evil in our own hearts and culture; it implies moving into a certain insecurity.

Belonging Breaking Down

Insecurity is, I think, at the heart of one of the great human dichotomies: the need for belonging and the need to be oneself, a real person, fully alive. In the fulfillment of the need for belonging is a certain surrender of the self to the group, the community, and the culture that provide a set of received truths. But to go further in the search for human fulfillment and inner freedom we need to reflect on the certitudes of the group, even to question them and take the risk of going against the grain.

It is when we act as individuals, allowing our deepest selves to arise, that what I call the principle of insecurity is most evident: we choose to live a certain insecurity and question things held to be true. However, to be insecure in this way is also, I believe, an important quality for the group or community; the things the group holds dear can be looked at, reflected on, questioned, and deepened, the better to find the truths contained therein. Let us look at this in more detail.

In many countries of the world, the family, the village,

and the tribe still remain strong; people feel bonded to one another. This bonding gives security; people know what to do and what to believe. Elders or leaders have a real power and authority. If someone falls sick, they are looked after. But there are disadvantages to such strong bonding. Members of the community sacrifice their individual consciousness and freedom at the altar of security and unity, the altar of bonding. For some, this submission can cause pain, particularly for those who are young and ambitious, who do not want to be enslaved in ancient traditions and in the collective poverty that is embraced by many such communities. The human urge is to liberate ourselves from what we perceive to be oppressive belonging. We want to find freedom but we want to find it within some kind of structure.

Among humankind, the family represents the basic social unit. However, everywhere we look, this basic place of belonging is breaking down. Let me take the country where I live, France, as an example. In Paris, one out of every two marriages ends in divorce and in the rest of France, one out of three goes the same way. Statistics show that everywhere, more and more people are frightened of commitment.

And why is this happening? I believe it is because our Western societies have placed the power, rights, and needs of the individual above those of the group. We have developed societies based on the principle of competition; people must work hard in order to succeed. Now, in a certain context, this can be healthy, particularly since a group can stifle both personal consciousness and freedom, as well as the development of one's gifts and capacities. Competition stretches our capacities but a focus on individual values and rights can push us into a terrible loneliness.

This is a loneliness that can bring some people, especially those who feel ill-equipped to live in the competitive world or who have never truly belonged in a family, to the depths of despair, where they lose their sense of self and of meaning. This is a place of insecurity at its most profound, insecurity in its most negative aspect.

But this loneliness can also cause us to seek out new ways of belonging, in places where we are helped to find a meaning for our lives, places where we may live out an ideal, where we may experience a true bonding with others. In the same way, this loneliness can cause us to search for new ways of bringing greater peace and justice to our society, to struggle with and for those who have been downtrodden, so that they may find an equitable place in society. This is a loneliness that will push some to seek new ways of healing the broken and those who cry out in pain; it will push others to seek truth and a new relationship with God.

A society based on the Darwinian "survival of the fittest," where we all fend for ourselves, has serious disadvantages. It promotes a strong, aggressive attitude and the need to win. It can paralyze the development of the heart, prevent healthy cooperation among people, and promote rivalry and enmity. It tends to marginalize those who are weak and even those who reject individualistic principles and want to live in and for a society based on truth and justice for all. In a society that encourages an ethics of

economy, of winning, and of power, it is important to be
admired. In such a society, an ethics of justice, solidarity,
and cooperation, an ethics of the common good, can
quickly fade into the background. Individual success is
all that matters. How can Western societies encourage
the development of personal consciousness, freedom,
and creativity and, at the same time, help us to not fall
into self-centred attitudes and motivations? How can we
orient the development of the individual towards works
of justice, the struggle for peace, and helping others to
develop their gifts and find their place in society?

Belonging That Closes Up

I think the answer lies in the way we might redefine the
place of the individual in the group and the place of
the group among other groups. As a society, we cannot
fail to recognize certain difficulties when the individual
is placed at the centre. A certain type of selfishness pre-
dominates, a selfishness that ill-serves the needs of the
larger whole.

We also need to find some way around the problem of
the group itself, the problem of competition that groups,
by their nature, seem to engender. It is easy to fall into
idealizing one's group and all its certitudes. It is easy, in
our weakness, to devolve individual moral responsibility
to the collective.

But here and there, there are, I believe, clues as to how
we may reformulate the notion of the group in ways that
will allow for the development of personal consciousness
and inner freedom. In this way, we become more fully

human, more fully alive: the healthy individual within the healthy group.

The history of civilization shows how men and women who want to commit themselves to a religious, cultural, or social ideal bond together to live out that vision, to find the structures that are necessary for what they want to do, and to give mutual support and care for each other. Such small groups have generally occurred within the world's great religions, where people come together with a common purpose. This is what we are trying to do in l'Arche as we build up small, family-sized communities. It is what many in our Western cultures sought to build during the 60s and 70s.

Let me give you some examples of what I consider healthy groups living in a deliberately chosen spirit of risk, adventure, courage, and openness. They live in what I call a spirit of insecurity, the embracing of an unknown future in an attitude of honest questioning.

In France, I regularly visit an enclosed convent where there are twenty-three women, young and old. They have come together to seek God, to give their lives to God, and to pray for all who suffer in the world. They live very poorly and work hard and the rule of life is quite fixed but they are very happy. They laugh and sing with ease. I find them very free and open in their hearts and minds, even though their convent is enclosed. They have found security in their life together but each one lives a personal insecurity. It is never easy to seek God, to be true in community life, and to accept others as they are — to forgive unceasingly, not hiding behind inner barriers.

A few years ago, I was invited to visit a group of "Jesus People" living in a depressed area of an American city. When I arrived in the large former hotel in which all the members live, I found them to be a community of about two hundred men and women, simply and poorly clothed, quite a few of them "punks" with coloured hair. As I spent time with them, I discovered that they gave free meals each day to some three hundred people who were down-and-out. I also realized that many of the members had suffered much, some through drugs and some through time spent in prison. I asked one of the leaders what their relations were with the mainstream churches of the city. He told me that, basically, no one wanted to accept them.

I found that group, which some might call a sect, quite beautiful. I was surprised by their openness. I was touched by how they were helping so many men and women to become more human.

That community functioned as a group, with common ideals and goals, but they welcomed the insecurity of their position as they embraced the insecurity of the down-and-out people they served. They were constantly remaking themselves. And it's probable that their embracing of change and their openness was actually fostered by the opposition they faced.

In some ways, these two groups, the convent in France and the "Jesus People" in the United States, are closed groups. Even though they are so different, one group facing in to the life of contemplation and the other facing out to the life of service, they are closed enough to give sufficient security to their members so that those people can live in insecurity and grow in love, openness, and compassion for others.

But communities that start out as healthy places of belonging can become too closed, rich, and elitist. What is the hunger for power that groups so readily acquire? Members come together to confirm each other's value. Communities can become like clubs for self-congratulation and flattery, status symbols of mediocrity. Rather than opening up to others, such groups close in on themselves. They lead to the death of the spirit.

Sometimes closedness is necessary, particularly in the initial stages. Some l'Arche communities, for example, were closed, to begin with, because they welcomed people with disabilities whose lives were totally unstructured and fragmented, people who were filled with such anguish, darkness, and confusion that it was impossible to have a dialogue with them. At first they needed to be told firmly what to do and sometimes they needed sanctions. Since they had never been respected or trusted, how could they, in turn, be expected to have respect and trust in themselves and in others?

Closed groups are found not only in religious and therapeutic circles but also in the political world, the military, multinational companies, hospitals, schools — all those places where people work together. In many organizations, individuals are expected to toe a certain line; there are norms governing behaviour. Every successful grouping of people in a common purpose has an articulated set of principles, a vision, a mission statement. An ideology, sometimes. Under such systems, individuals are encouraged not to think too much for themselves. Such systems encourage total obedience, cohesion, and efficiency; they are geared to obtaining, harnessing, and maintaining power in order to fulfill the mission, a mission which may be either philanthropic or commercial. Such groups, which have become a kind of basic unit in our society, insist more on belonging, cohesion, and the unity of the group than on the growth of individual members to inner freedom or service to others. Those who leave are seen as unfaithful; those who question authority, as rebels.

The most extreme example, perhaps, of closed groups, are what we call sects. Sects are initially seductive and attractive to very lonely and insecure people but, once they surrender their personal freedom and conscience, such people suffer the terrible fear of leaving the group. Outside, they could fall into even greater loneliness, insecurity, and anguish.

I bring up sects because, while most of us abhor the more extreme and obvious manifestations of sects, we can be blind to the innocuous sects that are a part of society. Our places of work, for example, can become like sects, where we have to sacrifice our personal consciences in order to keep our jobs, have a good salary, gain a measure of security. We need to be vigilant in any situation where it is necessary to obey blindly. Rigidity, a demand for ideological conformity within the group, is rarely necessary; it is not, I think, the sign of a healthy group. Not only that, but the price that we pay, as a society, in the repression of individual growth and the denigration of individual creativity, is too high.

Belonging for Growth Towards Maturity and Freedom

An individualism that manifests itself in doing things alone, in being concerned only with one's own interests and glory, one's own growth towards autonomy, competence, and power, is the antithesis of belonging. Such an individualism can grow out of anger towards an oppressive belonging, a demand to conform within a too-rigid group. It can come from a desire to become more fully oneself and to develop one's potential and personal consciousness. It can also come from a need to free oneself from all authority and all law in order to have more power and wealth. It is easy to forget that the sense of belonging is a necessary mediation between an individual and society. It is, above all, necessary to help us in our growth towards maturity and freedom.

Belonging is the fulcrum point for the individual between a sense of self and a sense of society. It is the rock on which we stand, in security, knowing who we are, capable of inner growth as we discover other realities born and developed in other groups and cultures.

Society is the place where we learn to develop our potential and become competent; where we work and receive a salary that allows us to live financially independently. It is the place where each can accomplish his or her mission, to work for justice, to struggle for peace, and to serve others.

Belonging, on the other hand, is the place where we can find a certain emotional security. It is the place where we learn a lot about ourselves, our fears, our blockages, and our violence, as well as our capacity to give life; it is the place where we grow to appreciate others, to live with them, to share and work together, discovering each one's gifts and weaknesses.

In healthy belonging, we have respect for one another. We work together, cooperate in a healthy way, listen to each other. We learn how to resolve the conflicts that arise when one person seeks to dominate another. In a true state of belonging, those who have less conventional knowledge, who are seemingly powerless, who have different capacities, are respected and listened to. In such a place of belonging, if it is a good place, power is not imposed from on high, but all members seek to work together as a body. The implication is that we see each other as persons and not just as cogs in a machine. We open up and interact with each other so that all can participate in the making of decisions.

This type of cooperation is not easy. It takes time to grow to a maturity of the heart. Belonging calls forth what is most beautiful in our capacity to love and accept others but it also can awaken anger, jealousy, violence, and the refusal to cooperate. This growth to maturity might mean that, at certain moments, authority has to be exercised with firmness. Little by little, as we live and work with others, especially if we are well-guided, we learn to break out of the shell of selfishness and self-centredness where we seek to be brilliant and to prove our goodness, wisdom, and power. We receive and give the knocks of life. It is like the polishing of diamonds as they rub together.

We all have to discover that there are others like us who have gifts and needs; no one of us is the centre of the world. We are a small but important part in our universe. We all have a part to play. We need one another.

It is because we belong with others and see them as brothers and sisters in humanity that we learn not only to accept them as they are, with different gifts and capacities, but to see each one as a person with a vulnerable heart. We learn to forgive those who hurt us or reject us; we ask forgiveness of those we have hurt. We learn to accept humbly those who point out our errors and mistakes and who challenge us to grow in truth and love. We support and encourage each other on the journey to inner freedom. We learn how to be close to those who are weaker and more vulnerable, those who may be sick or going through crises or are grieving. As we accept our personal limits and weaknesses, we discover that we need others and we learn to appreciate others and to thank them.

So it is that belonging is the place where we grow to maturity and discover what it means to be human and to act in a human way. It is the place we need in order to live and to act in society in justice, in truth, without seeking power, privileges, and honours for our own self-glory. It is the place where we learn to be humble but also audacious and to take initiatives in working with others. It is the place where our deepest self rises up into our consciousness and so we become more fully ourselves, more fully human.

The Jewish people have a deep sense of belonging. That is why when the prophet Isaiah saw his people going to the temple to fast and to make sacrifices but not open to those in distress, he cried out:

Is not this the sort of fast that pleases me?
To break unjust chains,
To undo the thongs of the yoke
and to let the oppressed go free?
Is it not sharing your food with the hungry,
and sheltering the homeless poor;
if you see someone lacking in clothes, to clothe them . . .

(Isaiah 58:6–7)

An openness to the weak and the needy in our own groups helps us to open our hearts to others who are weak and needy in the greater group of humanity. It is the first sign of a healthy group. A healthy bonding leads us to a greater love for others.

The second sign of healthy belonging is the way a group humbly lives its mission of service to others. It does not use or manipulate others for its own aggrandizement. It does not impose its vision on others but instead prefers to listen to what they are saying and living, to see in them all that is positive. It helps others to make their own decisions; it empowers them. When a community is closed and fearful of true dialogue where each person is respected, it is a sign of death not of life.

As we begin to see others' gifts, we move out from behind the walls of certitude that have closed us up, and this is the third sign of a healthy group. A few centuries ago, different Christian churches were fighting each other. Their theologies were calculated to prove that one was right and the other wrong. Today, instead of seeing what might separate us, whether as churches or cultures, we are instead seeing what unites us. We are beginning to see each other's gifts and to appreciate them and to realize that the important thing for each one of us is to grow in love and give of ourselves.

Fourth, it is a healthy sign when a group seeks to evolve and to recognize the errors of the past, to recognize its own flaws, and to seek the help of experienced people from outside the group in order to be more true and loving, more respectful of difference, more listening and open to the way authority is exercised. The group that refuses to admit its own errors or seek the wisdom of others risks closing itself up behind walls of "superiority."

Groups that develop with these four signs are, to my mind, healthy groups; they are helping their members to break free of the egotism inherent in us all and to grow towards greater maturity and inner freedom. They are discovering our common humanity, allowing us to be ourselves, intertwined with each other, receiving and giving life from one another. Do we not all share the same earth and sky? Are they not for us as we are for them? We all belong to each other, we are all for each other. God, too, is for us as we are for God. We are called to grow in order to become fully ourselves and fully alive, to receive from others, and to give to others, not being held back by fears, prejudices, or feelings of superiority or inferiority.

I believe that people can only get involved in the common good of a nation if they discover how we are all called to be people of service, of peace, and of justice. The common good is that which helps all to have a better life.

The historian and ecumenical theologian Donald Nicholl wrote extensively on many subjects. In particular, he had an enquiring mind about the role of the great religions as vehicles for interpreting God. In his provokingly truthful book, *The Beatitude of Truth*, he wrote about how the Catholic and Protestant churches in Nazi Germany were unable to rise up in support of the Jews persecuted by Hitler, even though they knew what was going on, even though they knew it was wrong. These churches had become closed in on themselves, they had lost sight of the larger principles to which they were committed.

In order for peace to come to our world, do not all nations need to discover that they are bonded together by a common destiny? By virtue of our belonging in the family of nations, we are all called to be concerned about others.

Belonging Together in a Pluralistic Society

Where does a broader sense of belonging come from? How do we break free of the straitjacket of group belonging? I believe it begins with human contact, with friendship, and as we listen to each other's stories.

We are all particularly touched when someone of another culture treats us kindly, even though we are not a member of their group, or when they reveal their inner pain, weakness, and difficulties. Perhaps it is then that we feel more deeply this bonding in a common humanity. Friendships grow between people of different backgrounds and cultures because they meet as persons, not because they share a common heritage. Such friendships grow because we all belong to the largest group of all, the human race.

Some religious people, on the other hand, see pluralistic societies, where people of different cultural and religious backgrounds meet and mix, as dangerous. They feel that religious values cannot be maintained in such societies.

The danger of moral corruption is real but there is also value when people begin to meet as members of humanity and not just as members of a group, as hearts meet hearts and people meet people outside of cultural and religious belonging. Prejudices begin to weaken as we discover that belonging to a group can foster illusions of superiority.

When religion closes people up in their own particular group, it puts belonging to the group, and its success and growth, above love and vulnerability towards others; it no longer nourishes and opens the heart. When this happens, religion becomes an ideology, that is to say, a series of ideas that we impose on ourselves, as well as on others; it closes us up behind walls. When religion helps us to open our hearts in love and compassion to those who are not of our faith so as to help them to find the source of freedom within their own hearts and to grow in compassion and love of others, then this religion is a source of life.

The heart is never "successful." It does not want power, honours, privilege, or efficiency; it seeks a personal relationship with another, a communion of hearts, which is the to-and-fro of love. This opening of the heart implies vulnerability and the offering of our needs and weaknesses. The heart gives and receives but above all, it gives. The heart goes out to those who are humble and who cry out in their weakness and their need for understanding and love. It is the human heart and its need for

communion that weakens the walls of ideology and prejudice. It leads us from closedness to openness, from the
illusion of superiority to vulnerability and humility.
Because of this, instead of finding security in the group,
we find it in our hearts, which have found a new inner
strength, a real maturity.

Closed and Open Groups

Sometimes the reason for coming together, the goal of the
community, can stifle personal relationships; individuals
no longer meet as persons, in heart-to-heart relationships,
but meet only as members of the same group, motivated
by the same goals. Some people, in fact, hide behind the
goals and activities of a group precisely in order to avoid
relationships. They see the value of others only as members of the group, sharing goals and ideals, and not as
individuals in themselves.

In l'Arche, we have begun to see the complexity of these
issues. In the early stages of community life, we did all we
could to strengthen the bonds among all the members.
This was done through community meetings and celebrations, religious services, times of prayer and of leisure
together, and, of course, through the attention that was
given to each individual. The intensity of community life
provides structure for people, helping them to find the
necessary intellectual and spiritual nourishment and to
live in security.

Such intense community life can, at the same time, cut
the community off from neighbours and society at large;
it can even prevent members from growing in autonomy,

personal freedom, responsibility, and inner maturity. Community life then becomes like a secure, "ideal" world, where the community is expected to look after all the needs of its members, until, of course, it breaks down due to the unfulfilled expectations and the inner conflicts that invariably arise.

However, if a community seeks total immersion in its surrounding area, it can lose its identity. Community members can become so intent on being one with their neighbours, on not being seen as different, that their sense of belonging, their sense of group identity, and, hence, their vision, gradually disappears. It is not easy to strike a balance between closedness, having a clear identity that fosters growth in certain values and spirituality, and openness to those who do not live with the same values. Isn't this the challenge of all religions and of all Christian churches? Being too open can dilute quality of life and stunt growth to maturity and wisdom; being too closed can stifle. It requires the wisdom, maturity, and inner freedom of community members to help the community find the harmony that not only preserves and deepens life and a real sense of belonging but also gives and receives life. Then the community has truly become an environment for becoming human, helping all to openness, freedom, and to commitment to the common good.

It is interesting in this respect to see how Jesus, who is the head and heart of all Christian faiths, responds to the question: Who is my neighbour? He does not talk about the person who lives nearby or the one who shares the same vision of life and of religion. He tells the story of a man who was walking from Jerusalem to Jericho and who was beaten up by thugs. As he lies in the road, those who are from his community, who might be expected to help him, pass by on the other side. A stranger, however, someone who belongs to another religious group, in fact, stops and cares for him. It is clearly this stranger, the good Samaritan, who sees the wounded man as a neighbour, who treats him as a neighbour, and who behaves as a neighbour should do. Throughout his life, Jesus taught and led people into a vision of our common humanity, where mercy and kindness are more important than ideology.

The Common Good: What Society?

It is in belonging that people discover what it means to be human. The breakdown of belonging, and the breakdown of the family, go hand in hand with the rise of anguish, of loneliness, and of chronic self-centredness. And here we find the roots of our great social unrest.

What are the factors in family, in school, and in society that will help us to live by moral values, to open up to the needs of others, to share with them and not just seek the most for ourselves and for our groups?

What we have lost, I think, is an understanding of belonging as a place of mediation.

A place of mediation is that place of belonging where we find structures and discipline, where we can search for truth together, where we find healing for our hearts that are incapable of relating to others in a healthy way, where we learn not to be locked up in our own needs and desires but to welcome others as they are, to accept that they have different gifts and capacities, that they are important and have value. The place of mediation helps us to discover that we are part of something much bigger, that together we can do something beautiful.

How to rekindle motivations that urge us to open up to others and to struggle to make our world a better place for all? Isn't it the duty of churches, religions, humanitarian organizations, social workers, schools of thought, and local governments to create situations, places of belonging and of dialogue, where we can discover that we can grow in love, find healing for our hearts, and do something worthwhile for others? Isn't it true that a change in society depends not only on the work of professionals but on each one of us working together? I am not sure what shape society should take in order for more and more people to be able to work together in greater mutual love and respect but I do know that such groups could become a light and a hope for the world.

It is only when there is a to-and-fro of ideas that we begin to feel listened to, included, valued. What is important is that each of us begins to trust in our own beauty and our capacity to do beautiful things and that we do not live simply in a struggle to survive, to achieve more in a competitive society. When we begin to believe that there is greater joy in working with and for others, rather than just for ourselves, then our society will truly become a place of celebration.

Belonging, then, is part of being human. The first and primary belonging is in family, where we find life and growth and acquire language, customs, culture, attitudes, and, in many ways, our psychological characteristics. Growth in human beings is like the growth of plants and of trees. We need to be rooted in earth, nourished by this earth and by the sun, water, and air in order to grow and to reach fulfillment, to bear fruit and give new life. If this "earth" is a place of language and a culture, it is essentially made up of people, people to whom we are bonded, committed people who love and appreciate us, people who call us forth to healthy relationships, openness, and love. Without other human beings, we close up in fear.

Our personalities deepen and grow as we live in openness and respect for others, when weakness is listened to and the weak are empowered, that is to say, when people are helped to be truly themselves, to own their lives and discover their capacity to give life to others. Fear closes us down; love opens us up.

In the next chapter, I will address the path of healing, from exclusion to inclusion and from fear to trust. Everything that is human needs nourishment: the body, the mind, the memory, the imagination, and, particularly, the heart. They must be nourished by encounters with other hearts that can lead us into other gardens of life, into a new and deeper vulnerability, and into a new understanding of the universe, of God, of history, and of the beauty and depth of each and every human being.

FROM EXCLUSION
TO INCLUSION:
A PATH OF HEALING

IN LUKE'S GOSPEL, Jesus tells a moving story. There was
a beggar named Lazarus who lived in the streets. He
was hungry and his legs were covered with sores. Living
opposite him, in a beautiful house, was a rich man who
used to give big parties for his friends. Lazarus would
have liked to have eaten some of the crumbs that fell from
his table but the dogs ate them up. One day, Lazarus died
and went to the place of peace, in the "heart of Abraham."
The rich man also died and he went to the "place of
torment." Looking up, he saw Lazarus radiant with peace
and he cried out: "Father Abraham please send Lazarus
down to put some water on my lips for I am in pain!"
Abraham responded: "It is impossible. Between you and
him there is an abyss that nobody can cross." He could
have added: "Just as there had been an abyss between
you and him during your life on earth."

This story of Lazarus tells us a lot about today's world,
where there is a huge abyss between those who have food,
money, and comfort and those who are hungry or have no

place of their own. I remember seeing children in Calcutta, their noses glued to the window of a luxurious restaurant. From time to time, the doorman would shoo them away. The rich — and that includes me and many of you who are reading this book — do not like to see dirty beggars staring at them. Haven't we all felt embarrassment and fear in front of those who are hungry?

One day in Paris, I was accosted by a rather dishevelled woman who shouted at me: "Give me some money!" We started to talk. I learned that she had just come out of a psychiatric hospital; I realized quite quickly that she had immense needs and I became frightened. I had an appointment and I didn't want to be late, so I gave her a little money and went on my way, just like the Pharisee and the Levite in the gospel parable of the good Samaritan. I was frightened of being swallowed up by her pain and her need.

What is this abyss that separates people? Why are we unable to look Lazarus straight in the eye and listen to him?

I suspect that we exclude Lazarus because we are frightened that our hearts will be touched if we enter into a relationship with him. If we listen to his story and hear his cry of pain we will discover that he is a human being. We might be touched by his broken heart and by his misfortunes. What happens when our hearts are touched? We might want to do something to comfort and help him, to alleviate his pain, and where will that lead us? As we enter into dialogue with a beggar, we risk entering into an adventure. Because Lazarus needs not only money but also a place to stay, medical treatment, maybe work, and, even more, he needs friendship.

That is why it is dangerous to enter into a relationship with the Lazaruses of our world. If we do, we risk our lives being changed.

All of us are, more or less, locked up in our cultures, in our habits, even in our friendships and places of belonging. If I become the friend of a beggar, I rock the boat. Friends may feel uncomfortable, even threatened, by my new ways; perhaps they feel challenged to do likewise. They may become aggressive, they may criticize the foolish, so-called utopian ways of the one in their midst who befriends a beggar.

I am beginning to discover how fear is a terrible motivating force in all our lives. We are frightened of those who are different. We are frightened of failure and of rejection. And I have become increasingly aware not only of my own fears but of the fears of others. Fear is at the root of all forms of exclusion, just as trust is at the root of all forms of inclusion.

The history of humanity is a history of wars, oppression, slavery, and rejection. Every society in every time has created its own forms of exclusion.

There is an endless list of those whom we may exclude; every one of us, we may be sure, is on someone's list: the homeless, the sick, the dying, the young, the old, the weak, the disabled, the stranger, the immigrant, those with AIDS . . .

My experience of exclusion has been mainly with those who have intellectual disabilities. I have visited abominable institutions all over the world. In African countries, I have seen men and women considered "mad" chained to trees, beaten until they bled in order to liberate the so-called devil that possessed them. In Latin America, I have visited an asylum where about one hundred men and women, most of them half naked, shared a collapsing building with large black and white rats.

But this form of physical mistreatment is only one manifestation of a wider exclusion.

I have come to the conclusion that those with intellectual disabilities are among the most oppressed and excluded people in the world. Even their own parents are frequently ashamed to have given birth to a child "like that." Such parents feel humiliated and ashamed by the apparent failure, so great is the social pressure to create a perfect baby.

In some cultures, children with disabilities are seen as a punishment from God. In the ninth chapter of John's gospel, the disciples question Jesus about a beggar who was born blind: "Was it because of his sins or the sins of his parents that he was born blind?" they ask. This feeling of guilt is found in many cultures. A doctor in France came to speak to me about his eleven-year-old daughter who had a disability. He told me that, at her birth, when he noticed she had a disability, his immediate reaction was: "What have I done to God that he should send me such a disaster?" It is not easy to live with such feelings of guilt.

Fear at the Basis of
Prejudice and Exclusion

I have been living for more than thirty years with men and women who have been excluded from society. I have seen firsthand how fear is a great and terrible motivator of human actions. Through my experience with these men and women with intellectual disabilities, I have become more aware of how fear is at the heart of prejudice and exclusion.

We are all frightened of those who are different, those who challenge our authority, our certitudes, and our value system. We are all so frightened of losing what is important for us, the things that give us life, security, and status in society. We are frightened of change and, I suspect, we are even more frightened of our own hearts.

Fear makes us push those with intellectual disabilities into far-off, dismal institutions. Fear prevents all of us with the price of a meal in our pocket from sharing with the Lazaruses of the world. It is fear, ironically, that prevents us from being most human, that is, it prevents us from growing and changing. Fear wants nothing to change; fear demands the status quo. And the status quo leads to death.

Fear always seeks an object. If I feel insecure in myself, I will almost always find some scapegoat for my fear, someone or something that I can turn into the object of my fear and then my anger. But there are some broad categories for the objects of fear, and I think it's worth looking at some of them.

Fear of Dissidents

First of all, there is the fear of dissidents. There has always been a fear of the dissident, that is to say, of the one who seems to threaten the existing order. Those who fear the dissident are those who have a vested interest in the maintenance of that order; frequently, money and power, or the need to control others and to feel superior to them, are at the root of such interests. When political leaders — kings, most frequently — were seen as the representatives of God on earth, protectors of truth, religion, and morality then whoever opposed such leaders were necessarily regarded as evil, agents of the devil. If the status quo was ordained by God, whoever stood against the status quo stood against God and the natural order. The appeal to "God on our side" was always a powerful justification for torture and killing in the name of truth.

The millions who were tortured and eliminated in Stalin's Russia, in German concentration camps, in South Africa, Guatemala, Chile, any one of a hundred countries in our own time, were seen, in all sincerity, as evil and dangerous by those they opposed. Dictators have always maintained an elaborate secret police to exclude and suppress those who oppose them.

The story of humanity is that of heroes and martyrs with a new vision for humanity, regarded as terrorists and dissidents by some, as prophets of freedom by others. Christians were thrown to wild beasts in the coliseum because the Romans saw this new, strange religion as a threat to the existing order.

It is in the nature of power to resist change; the principle of the divine right of kings goes back at least as far as the first man — and it probably was a man — who sought to establish the continuity of his power as a natural law. We live in a more secular time but we have transformed the divine right of kings into the divine right of anybody in power.

There is a deeper issue here, beyond the self-aggrandizement of the powerful. Leaders consider themselves as generally in the right. It is part of the paradigm we have created: if you have succeeded in making your way to the top, then, by definition, by the law of natural selection, the values for which you stand have been authenticated. That is why it always seems entirely reasonable for the powerful to seek to quell and exclude anyone who opposes them. Those who oppose create disorder; they run against the natural order.

The only point to be made about all this is that it is important for leaders to listen to dissent and try to understand where it is coming from and what is true in it. If history teaches us nothing else, it is that power is borrowed. At best, power is something granted not something taken. That means, in Western democracies at any rate, that those who have power need the gifts of discernment and judgement, because if we recognize the temporary nature of power, then equally, we need to recognize what in the activity of dissent is valuable.

The principle at issue is the temporary nature of power, and the necessity of service and humility, the necessity of seeing what truth is being cried out in an act of protest.

FEAR OF DIFFERENCE

Second, there is the fear of difference. In the last chapter, I tried to show how belonging can be a stepping stone to life but how it can also stifle and actually prevent life. Human nature is to want to belong to groups of like-minded creatures, to those of the same culture or who have the same goals and interests. If we know each other, we can work together. We feel safe together. Those who are different disturb us.

Who are those who are different? They are the people who suffer poverty, brokenness, disabilities, or loneliness. They cry out to us for help, these millions named Lazarus. Often, they are in discomfort while others live in comfort. Their cries become dangerous for those of us who live in comfort. If we listen to their cries and open up our hearts, it will cost us something. So we pretend not to hear the cry and so exclude them.

Those who are different are the strangers among us. There are many ways of being different: one can be different by virtue of values, culture, race, language or education, religious or political orientation. And while most of us can find it stimulating or at least interesting to meet a stranger for a short while, it is a very different thing to truly open up and allow a stranger to become a friend.

This fear of the different is very marked when it comes to people with intellectual disabilities. I remember when I first met such people. Father Thomas Philippe, the French priest who became my spiritual accompanier when I left the navy and who was instrumental in the founding of l'Arche, invited me to meet his "new friends" in a small institution where he was the chaplain. At the time, I was teaching philosophy at St. Michael's College in Toronto. I accepted his invitation but, nevertheless, I was very anxious. How was I going to communicate with people who could not talk? If they could talk, what would we talk about? I was fearful of not being able to cope with the situation or of not knowing what to do and of being inadequate.

When we have constructed our lives around particular values of knowledge, power, and social esteem, it is difficult for us to accept those who cannot live by the same set of values. It is as if we are threatened by such people.

The social stigmas around people with intellectual disabilities are strong. There is an implicit question: If someone cannot live according to the values of knowledge and power, the values of the greater society, we ask ourselves, can that person be fully human?

People with intellectual disabilities are generally placed at the lowest end of the human spectrum. When I first encountered them at l'Arche, I believed in love but, for me, love meant generosity, doing good for others. At that time, I did not realize that through our love we can help others to discover their own intrinsic value; we can reveal to them their beauty and their uniqueness.

Gradually, through l'Arche, I began to see the value of the communion of hearts and of a love that empowers, that helps others to stand up; a love that shows itself in humility and in trust. If our society has difficulty in functioning, if we are continually confronted by a world in crisis, full of violence, of fear, of abuse, I suggest it is because we are not clear about what it means to be human. We tend to reduce being human to acquiring knowledge, power, and social status. We have disregarded the heart, seeing it only as a symbol of weakness, the centre of sentimentality and emotion, instead of as a powerhouse of love that can reorient us from our self-centredness, revealing to us and to others the basic beauty of humanity, empowering us to grow.

FEAR OF FAILURE

We have talked about fear of dissidents and fear of difference; another fear that drives us is the fear of failure.

The fear of failure, of feeling helpless and unable to cope, had been built up in me ever since my childhood. I had to be a success. I had to prove my worth. I had to be right. This need to succeed and to be accepted, even admired by my parents and by those whom I considered my "superiors," was a strong motivating force in me and is a motivation at the heart of many human endeavours.

The urge to please and to succeed is obviously a valuable motivation but it has its flip side. Not everyone can succeed at the same entrance exam; many must fail. And failure can and does break people. This need to succeed, coupled with the fear of failure and the fear of being rejected and of falling into loneliness and anguish, can make us choose to relate only to those who like and admire us: those who look on us as winners. And, of course, we recognize others playing the same game.

People with intellectual disabilities, however, seem so different, as if they were in another world; it seems impossible to communicate easily with them. We can feel totally helpless in front of them.

Fear of failure, of not coping with a situation, of not being able to relate to another person, is at the heart of this fear of the different, the strange, the stranger. It is as if we are walking in unknown territory.

FEAR OF LOSS AND CHANGE

Then there is the fear of loss and change. Why do the rich and powerful — you and I, in short — fear so much the Lazaruses in our midst? Is it not because we are frightened of having to share our wealth, frightened of losing something? It is easy to give a few coins to a beggar; it is more difficult to give what is necessary to maintain our own standard of living. We feel so inadequate in the face of poverty. What can we do to change so many seemingly impossible situations? When I rushed away from that woman in Paris who had just come out of a psychiatric hospital, it was because I did not really know what to do, what was appropriate; I had this fear of being sucked into a vortex of poverty. To be open is an enormously risky enterprise; you risk status, power, money, even friendship, the recognition and sense of belonging that we so prize; you risk the chaos of loneliness.

For a number of years, a married couple, friends of mine, were close with a number of other couples. The group was concerned with the increasing gap between the rich and the poor in their city and they wanted to do something about it. My friends became impatient with all the discussion and they decided to do something alone. They left

the group and went to live in a poor area of the city. The
others in the group saw them as "traitors" to the group
and shunned them. To me this is a reminder that when we
get committed to those who are excluded or marginalized,
we run the risk of being criticized by our family and
friends. To leave the culture of friends and family is like
going into another world.

We all need a certain amount of security in order to be
able to live peacefully. This sense of security comes from
the way we live our lives; it comes from the presence of
and reinforcement from family and friends; it comes from
our place of work and through daily routines. In this
context, the unexpected can provoke a crisis. To lose the
"known" and to move on to the "unknown" can mean a
terrible loss for us. To live such loss one needs a great deal
of inner strength.

To give food to a beggar who knocks on the door can be
quite an easy thing to do. But if he keeps coming back —
with his friends — then what do we do? We can become
totally lost and insecure. We are at sea with no horizon, in
unknown territory without a map. We are frightened that
the beggar is calling on us to change our lifestyle.

We are all frightened of the ugly, the dirty. We all want
to turn away from anything that reveals the failure, pain,
sickness, and death beneath the brightly painted surface
of our ordered lives. Civilization is, at least in part, about
pretending that things are better than they are. We all
want to be in a happy place, where everyone is nice and
good and can fend for themselves. We shun our own
weakness and the weakness in others. We refuse to listen

to the cry of the needy. How easy it is to fall into the illusion of a beautiful world when we have lost trust in our capacity to make of our broken world a place that can become more beautiful.

THE ORIGIN OF THESE FEARS

What is the origin of the terrible fears that so hinder us in the making of our heart's desire: a better world?

I believe that the origins of fear of dissidence and of the different, of failure and of loss, as well as the fear of the ugly and the dirty, are to be found in the fears experienced in childhood. Parents can make their children feel that they have to merit their love, that it is a reward for good behaviour. Children, under these conditions, feel that they have to be perfect, match up to their parents' norms before love is deserved. Worth is something to be proved; the unique value of each person is not acknowledged to be an intrinsic quality.

In his book, *Le Chemin de l'homme*, or *The Road of Mankind*, the Jewish philosopher Martin Buber says that "with each person who comes into the world, there is something new that has never existed before, something totally new and unique. . . . It is this unique and exceptional quality that each person is called to develop."[1]

But how can children feel they are unique if they have to fit their parents' norms? It is only when children are accepted as they are, with their unique gifts and limits, when they are listened to and respected, that they will be able later on to accept others. Love and respect, like fear and prejudice, are legacies passed on from one person to another. The movement from seeking approval to taking responsibility, to being open to those who are different, implies a shift of consciousness. It is as if a shell is broken and, gradually, the real person is able to emerge.

One major reason for our mutual distrust, for our propensity to gang together in mutually exclusive groups, is that most of us experience love in only the most imperfect way. When I discover that I am accepted and loved as a person, with my strengths and weaknesses, when I discover that I carry within myself a secret, the secret of my uniqueness, then I can begin to open up to others and respect their secret. The fear of others begins to dissolve; inclusion, friendship, and a feeling of brotherhood/sisterhood begins to emerge. As we become more conscious of the uniqueness of others, we become aware of our common humanity. We are all fundamentally the same, no matter what our age, gender, race, culture, religion, limits, or disabilities may be. We all have vulnerable hearts and need to be loved and appreciated. We have all been wounded in our hearts and have lost trust in what is deepest in us. We all want to be valued and to be able to develop our capacities and grow to greater freedom.

Until we realize that we belong to a common humanity, that we need each other, that we can help each other, we will continue to hide behind feelings of elitism and superiority and behind the walls of prejudice, judgement, and disdain that those feelings engender.

Each human being, however small or weak, has something to bring to humanity. In our beautiful universe, there are suns and stars, as well as the multitude of small animals and plants that are important because of their beauty, their healing qualities, and their capacity to give life. Every part of the body is important and has a role to play in our overall well-being.

In the same way, each person, big or small, has a role to play in the world. As we start to really get to know others, as we begin to listen to each other's stories, things begin to change. We no longer judge each other according to concepts of power and knowledge or according to group identity, but according to these personal, heart-to-heart encounters. We begin the movement from exclusion to inclusion, from fear to trust, from closedness to openness, from judgement and prejudice to forgiveness and understanding. It is a movement of the heart. We begin to see each other as brothers and sisters in humanity. We are no longer governed by fear but by the heart.

From Exclusion to Inclusion

How do we move from exclusion to inclusion?

When I talk about "inclusion" of people, whether they are those with disabilities, beggars like Lazarus, or people suffering from AIDS, I am not talking only about starting up special schools or residences or creating good soup kitchens or new hospitals. These are, of course, necessary. I am not just saying that we should be kind to such people because they are human beings. Nor is it a question of "normalizing" them in order that they can be "like us," participate in church services, and go to the movies and the local swimming pool. When I speak of the inclusion of those who are marginalized I am affirming that they have a gift to give to all, to each of us as individuals, to the larger forms of human organization, and to society, in general.

The excluded, I believe, live certain values that we all need to discover and to live ourselves before we can become truly human. It is not just a question of performing good deeds for those who are excluded but of being open and vulnerable to them in order to receive the life that they can offer; it is to become their friends. If we start to include the disadvantaged in our lives and enter into heartfelt relationships with them, they will change things in us. They will call us to be people of mutual trust, to take time to listen and be with each other. They will call us out from our individualism and need for power into belonging to each other and being open to others. They will break down the prejudices and protective walls that gave rise to exclusion in the first place. They will then start to affect our human organizations, revealing new ways of being and walking together.

So, the one-way street, where those on top tell those at the bottom what to do, what to think, and how to be, becomes a two-way street, where we listen to what they, the "outsiders," the "strangers," have to say and we accept what they have to give, that is, a simpler and more profound understanding of what it means to be truly human.

If we start to see people at the bottom as friends, as people with gifts to bring to others, then the social pyramid, with the powerful, the knowledgeable, and the wealthy on top, becomes a place of belonging where each person finds their place and where we live in mutual trust.

Is this a utopian vision? If it is lived at the grassroots level, in families, communities, and other places of belonging, this vision can gradually permeate our societies and humanize them.

I'm not suggesting for a moment that each one of us must welcome into our homes all those who are marginalized. I am suggesting that if each one of us, with our gifts and weaknesses, our capacities and our needs, opens our heart to a few people who are different and become their friends, receive life from them, our societies would change. This is the way of the heart.

The Heart

The heart, the metaphorical heart, the basis of all relationships, is what is deepest in each one of us. It is my heart that bonds itself to another heart; it leads us out of the restricted belonging, which creates exclusion, to meet and love others just as they are. A little child is only heart; he thrives off relationships; his joy is in relationships; he grows through relationships. When he is in communion with someone he trusts, he is safe, he is someone, someone unique and important. He is thus empowered, for the rest of his life, to be open to others, and to bring this sense of empowerment into his work.

To work means to be energetic, strong, and active, cooperating with others. Communion means to be vulnerable and tender; it means opening one's heart and sharing one's hopes and pain, even all that is failure or brokenness.

If my heart is broken, I can quickly feel crushed and fall into depression, unable to work. Or, I may refuse all relationships and throw myself savagely into work. If my heart is fulfilled, it will shine through my work.

We've all seen the transforming power of love. The most hardened, embittered person sees themselves and sees life in a new way when they fall in love and when they know that they are loved. It is easy to recognize a man or a woman in love. Aggressive or depressive tendencies seem to disappear. They move towards a gentle openness. Instead of protecting themselves behind barriers, they make themselves open and welcoming. A new freedom, kindness, and tenderness become evident.

My point is that a human being is more than the power or capacity to think and to perform. There is a gentle person of love hidden in the child within each adult. The heart is the place where we meet others, suffer, and rejoice with them. It is the place where we can identify and be in solidarity with them. Whenever we love, we are not alone. The heart is the place of our "oneness" with others.

The way of the heart implies a choice. We can choose to take this path and to treat people as people and not just as machines. We can see the cook in a hotel simply as somebody who is paid to cook well or as a person with a heart, who has children, and who might be living painful relationships and is in need of understanding and kindness. To treat each person as a person means that we are concerned for them, that we listen to them, and love them and want them to become more whole, free, truthful, and responsible.

To speak of the heart is not to speak of vaguely defined emotions but to speak of the very core of our being. At the core, we all know we can be strengthened and rendered more truthful and more alive. Our hearts can become hard like stone or tender like flesh. We have to create situations where our hearts can be fortified and nourished. In this way, we can be more sensitive to others, to their needs, their cries, their inner pain, their tenderness, and their gifts of love.

Our hearts, however, are never totally pure. People can cry out to be loved, especially if as children they were not loved. There are "loving" relationships that are unhealthy because they are a flight from truth and from responsibility. There are friendships that are unhealthy because one is too frightened to challenge one's friend. These are the signs of the immature heart. An immature heart can lead us to destructive relationships and then to depression and death.

It is only once a heart has become mature in love that it can take the road of insecurity, putting its trust in God. It is a heart that can make wise decisions; it has learned to discern and to take risks that bring life. It can meet other people inside and outside of the place of belonging. It can meet people who have been excluded. It is the heart that helps us to discover the common humanity that links us all, that is even stronger than all that bonds us together as part of a specific group. The heart, then, foregoes the need to control others. The free heart frees others.

Heart-to-heart relationships where God is present are more important than the approbation of society or of a group. Belonging to a group is important; it is the "earth" in which we grow. Sometimes we have to forego group approval and even accept rejection, if it should happen, in order to follow what the ancients called "scientia cordis," the science of the heart, which gives the inner strength to put truth, flowing from experience, over the need for approval. The science of the heart permits us to be vulnerable with others, not to fear them but to listen to them, to see their beauty and value, to understand them in all their fears, needs, and hopes, even to challenge them if need be. It permits us to accept others just as they are and to believe that they can grow to greater beauty. The mature heart does not seek to force belief on others; it does not seek to impose a faith. The mature heart listens for what another's heart is called to be. It no longer judges or condemns. It is a heart of forgiveness. Such a heart is a compassionate heart that sees the presence of God in others. It lets itself be led by them into unchartered land. It is the heart that calls us to grow, to change, to evolve, and to become more fully human.

The Way of the Heart

I discovered the "way of the heart" in l'Arche, as a way of putting people first, of entering into personal relationships. This way of approaching each individual, of relating to each one with gentleness and kindness was not easy for me. I joined the navy when I was very young, just thirteen, a highly impressionable age. All my training was geared to help me to be quick, competent, and efficient, and so I became. As a naval officer, and even later, after I had left the navy, I was a rather stiff person, geared to goals of efficiency, duty, prayer, and doing good to others and to philosophical and theological studies. My energies were goal-oriented.

From the beginning, in 1964, l'Arche has been truly a learning experience for me. It has brought me into the world of simple relationships, of fun and laughter. It has brought me back into my body, because people with disabilities do not delight in intellectual or abstract conversation. There are times when, of course, conversation with them is serious; we need to talk about fundamental realities of life such as birth, death, sexuality, prayer, and justice. They need times of work where they can see what they can accomplish. Leisure times are centred around fun, games, and celebrations. Theirs is not a life centred on the mind. So it is that the people with intellectual disabilities led me from a serious world into a world of celebration, presence, and laughter: the world of the heart.

When we are in communion with another, we become open and vulnerable to them. We reveal our needs and our weaknesses to each other. Power and cleverness call forth admiration but also a certain separation, a sense of distance; we are reminded of who we are not, of what we cannot do. On the other hand, sharing weaknesses and needs calls us together into "oneness." We welcome those who love us into our heart. In this communion, we discover the deepest part of our being: the need to be loved and to have someone who trusts and appreciates us and who cares least of all about our capacity to work or to be clever and interesting. When we discover we are loved in this way, the masks or barriers behind which we hide are dropped; new life flows. We no longer have to prove our worth; we are free to be ourselves. We find a new whole-ness, a new inner unity.

I love to watch little children playing and chatting among themselves. They do not care what people think. They do not have to try to appear to be clever and impor-tant. They know they are loved and are free to be them-selves. As they grow into adolescence and adulthood, they become more self-conscious. They lose a certain freedom, which they may find again later, when they rediscover that they are loved and accepted just as they are and are no longer obsessed by what others may think of them.

Spiritual masters in sacred scripture often tell stories to reveal truths and to awaken hearts. Jesus spoke in par-ables; Hasidic Jews and Sufi teachers tell tales; Hindu scripture is full of stories. Stories seem to awaken new energies of love; they tell us great truths in simple, personal terms and make us long for light. Stories have a strange power of attraction. When we tell stories, we touch hearts. If we talk about theories or speak about ideas, the mind may assimilate them but the heart remains untouched.

To witness is to tell our story. In l'Arche, we love to tell our stories and how people with disabilities have trans-formed us, stories that reveal their love and simplicity and that speak of their courage, pain, and closeness to God. It is hard to be interesting if we speak in general terms about those with disabilities; people are not always terri-bly interested. It is the story of a specific person that touches the listener.

When we hear stories of others who have lived as we

have lived and how they have risen up from the drab and found hope, we, too, find hope. Stories of transformation from death to life sow seeds of hope.

Let me tell some stories.

First, let me tell you about Antonio, who has brought many people into the way of the heart. Antonio came to our community in Trosly when he was twenty years old, after many years in hospital. He could not walk, speak, or use his hands; he needed extra oxygen to breathe. He was a weak and fragile man in many ways but he had an incredible smile and beautiful shining eyes. There was no anger or depression in him. That is not to say that he didn't get annoyed from time to time, especially if his bathwater was too hot or too cold or if the assistants forgot about him! What is important is that he had accepted his limits and disabilities; he had accepted himself just as he was. Antonio could not love by being generous, by giving things to people or by doing things for them; he himself was too needy. He lived a love of trust. In this way, he touched many people's hearts. When one loves with trust, one does not give things, one gives oneself and, so, calls forth a communion of hearts.

Antonio touched and awakened the hearts of many assistants who came to live in his house. He led them into the way of the heart. Often, they would tell me so, in words to this effect: "Antonio has changed my life. He led me out of a society of competition where one has to be strong and aggressive into a world of tenderness and mutuality, where each person, strong or weak, can exercise their gifts."

I recently received a letter that read, in part: "Two weeks ago my brother died. He was my oldest brother. Six years ago he had a heart attack which left him brain damaged. He spent the last years of his life in a nursing home. At his funeral many nurses and staff came and expressed such intense grief that I was profoundly moved. Six years ago, when my brother was struggling with death, I was angry with God. How could this be a life for someone who dreaded so much ending up as he did? Peter gave so much to others in his final years. One nurse told me: 'I always went to see Peter when I was feeling down and his spirit would lift up my spirits.'"

What actually happened to these assistants when they entered into a heart-to-heart relationship with Antonio or other people like him? What did Peter do to the nurse? People like Antonio and Peter are masters at teaching the way of the heart. For them as for children or elderly people who have lost some of their faculties, abstract, rational language, cut off from affectivity, is beyond their reach; the way of the heart is the only way in which they can communicate.

Henri Nouwen was a Dutch priest who gave many years of his life to Daybreak, the l'Arche community near Toronto. He was a spiritual guide to many in our community and, through his books, to many outside, as well. In one of his last books, *Adam*, he talks about how his life was transformed through his contact with a man who had severe physical and intellectual disabilities.

Here is the man who more than anyone connected me with my inner self, my community and my God. Here is the man I was asked to care for, but who took me into his life and his heart in such an incredibly deep way. Here is my counselor, my teacher, my guide, who could never say a word to me but taught me more than any book, professor or spiritual director.[2]

Freedom from Conformity

A few years ago, a number of people from our communities went on a pilgrimage to Rome. We had an audience with Pope John Paul II. While we were waiting for him to arrive, Fabio, a young man with disabilities, walked up and sat down in the Pope's chair. It was obviously the best chair in the room, which is why Fabio felt so attracted to it. Bishops who were close by did not know what to do. An assistant, however, helped Fabio find another chair that was quite good, too!

I would never have dared to do what Fabio did. Like many of us, I tend to conform to what is expected of me and am fearful of going against the norm or of what my "superiors" want of me. Is there a fear in me of being seen as guilty if I go against the norm? Or am I fearful of someone shouting at me angrily?

Some people like to rock the boat, to do the unexpected, unusual thing just to shock others and draw their attention. People with disabilities, however, do not go against the norm to shock others. It is just their way of being, flowing from their intuitive sense of inner freedom.

People with disabilities have a freedom to get angry and then to ask for forgiveness when they realize they have hurt someone. Then it is finished. There is no smouldering fire ready to flare up again at the least provocation. The authenticity of their contrition always touches me.

Is it because they have little awareness of time and history, of the moral bridle that memory places on our actions? It is the remembrance of things past and of the previous consequences of our actions that governs many of our present actions. Many of those with intellectual disabilities, however, are not people of the past or even of the future but of the present moment. They have no big plans for tomorrow. Plans are more for people who have greater autonomy and the capacity to lead their lives as they want. Those with disabilities do not cry out for power or success; their energies are used for seeking out the warmth of relationships. I notice how many of us have our eye on the clock, mindful of our next meeting, a talk to give, deadlines to meet. People with intellectual disabilities do not seem to be governed by time in the same way. They tend to live more fully in the present, sometimes enjoying themselves, sometimes angry, usually trusting in the presence of people who appreciate them.

Prejudices Fall

When assistants arrive in our communities, they are often filled with the prejudices of the competitive society to which they belong. Then they discover Antonio, with his heart of love, his gentleness, his acceptance of self, and his abandonment to the present moment, hidden behind the weakness and brokenness of his body. They then realize more fully the intolerance, the lack of love, and even the cruelty of their culture and maybe even of their church. They begin to realize that to become fully human is not a question of following what everyone else does, of conforming to social norms, or of being admired and honoured in a hierarchical society; it is to become free to be more fully oneself, to follow one's deepest conscience, to seek truth, and to love people as they are.

The point of inclusion is the belief that each of us is important, unique, sacred, in fact. We can only relate to others and begin to include them in our lives and our society if we have this primary belief. That means that we bring each other to birth as we respect and love one another and as our value is revealed to us through the love of others. We close up if we are seen as having no value. Justice means more than just following the law, not hurting people; it also means respecting and valuing each individual.

Justice flows from the heart. If human beings are crying out for justice, if we are all deeply moved by deeds of injustice, do not our cries reveal our humanity? Our basic needs are the same as those of all other human beings. We need other people who will call forth what is most beautiful in us, just as we need to call forth what is most beautiful in others.

When we enter into a personal relationship with those who are different or on the fringes of society, it is amazing how we are able to look more critically at our own culture. We begin to see the deep prejudices that exist. Let me give you an example.

Not long ago, I met a man who had come to our community quite a few years ago. He is from an Algerian family and has a slight intellectual disability. Because of his abilities, and because he worked hard, he was able to find a job and to live on his own. We met each other at the train station and travelled to Paris together. Being with him, I noticed how sensitive I was to the way people looked at him; I could feel when there was fear or dislike in their eyes because of his North African features.

When we ally ourselves with the excluded in society, not only are we enabled to see people as people and to join them in their struggle for justice, to work for community and places of belonging, but we also develop the critical tools for seeing what is wrong in our own society.

This lowering of inner barriers, which are our prejudices, is an important factor in our growth towards personal freedom. It's not easy to cast a critical eye on our own culture. Individual identity is so linked to culture that any form of critical judgement in this respect can endanger the stability of our inner world. We are like children who have put all their trust in their parents but, when we see our parents doing wrong, our inner world collapses, we lose our reference points and feel lost. Wisdom grows when we cast a critical eye not only on ourselves but also on the group to which we belong. It is only then that we begin to want to work for change.

Becoming a friend to a marginalized, excluded person is an act of self-imposed exile from most of the world. It is liberating, an act of freedom. It is a path to personal growth where one proclaims a new set of values. It is the first step towards living new values but it does not in itself constitute a transformation.

To Become Human

Xavier Lepichon is a well-known French geologist, member of the Académie des Sciences, and professor at the Collège de France. In his fascinating book, *Aux Racines de l'homme*, or *The Roots of Humanity*, he shows that, throughout the different stages of the evolution of humanity, people have become more human as they opened up to the weak and to the reality of suffering and death. That is also my personal experience. As the human heart opens up and becomes compassionate, we discover our fundamental unity, our common humanity.

It seems paradoxical to say that people with disabilities have taught me what it means to be human and that they are leading me into a new vision of society, a more human society. With and through them I have discovered the joys of celebration, love, working, and communicating together in mutual respect and in laughter. I realize more deeply how spirituality flows from being human, or rather how spirituality is being fully human and so shapes our lives and our humanity. I have discovered the value of psychology and psychiatry, that their teachings can undo knots in us and permit life to flow again and aid us in becoming more truly human. I have myself experienced how religion can open us up to the universe, to the love of all humanity, and, especially, to the source of all life and love, to a meeting with God. This meeting with God, I find, is not first and foremost for those who are most clever and honourable but for those who are weak and humble and open to love, for those who take the way of the heart.

Simplicity

Tenderness is the language of the body as a mother holds her child, as a nurse touches the patient's wound, or as an assistant bathes someone with severe disabilities. Recently, in a Buddhist monastery, I watched a sister as she served us food and tea with great delicacy; it was as if the meal itself was sacred, revealing a presence of God. And so it did, because it was treated so. Tenderness is the language of the body speaking of respect; thus, the body honours whatever it touches; it honours reality. It does not act as if reality itself must be changed or possessed; reality belongs to humanity and to God. Isn't this the way we should relate to all living beings — plants, animals, and the earth?

Isaiah writes about the Messiah:

> He will not cry or lift up his voice,
> or make it heard on the street;
> a bruised reed he will not break
> and a flickering wick he will not quench.

> (Isaiah 42:2–3)

There is no fear in tenderness. Tenderness is not weakness, lack of strength, or sloppiness; tenderness is filled with strength, respect, and wisdom. In tenderness, we know how and when to touch someone to help them to *be* and to be well. Through my contact with Raphael and Philippe, the first two people I welcomed to l'Arche, and my many, many other teachers among the people with disabilities, I have in some small way learned to inhabit my body and to see it not just as a channel for therapy but as a way of revealing my heart and of being in communion with others.

I have alluded to the way in which communion has the power to reveal beauty and value to another, how it frees us to be truly ourselves, but this communion demands respectful listening to the nonverbal language of the other person. I say nonverbal because, in the world of friendship and relationship, gestures normally precede the word. The word is there to confirm the gesture and give it its signification.

I see now that this communion with people with disabilities, and the tenderness implied, has helped me to find a new inner wholeness, a unity between my affectivity and my intelligence.

The way of the heart is the path to healing our deepest affectivity and needs, through communion and the gift of self. This healing, however, is never perfectly accomplished. There will always be a struggle. But if we are vigilant and prayerful, centred on truth and not seduced by riches, power, publicity, pleasure, and other psychological needs, then we will be able to continue on the path of healing. I am grateful to those with disabilities who have led me to this way of the heart, which is the road to healing.

Acceptance of Self

Antonio taught many of us at l'Arche the need to accept ourselves just as we are. Even though he was so weak and fragile, suffering from multiple disabilities, he was truly a man of joy. This joy flowed through his smiling eyes and face, revealing an inner peace and serenity.

Those of us with power and social standing have subtle ways of hiding our inner handicaps, our difficulties in relationships, our inner darkness and violence, our depression and lack of self-confidence. When all is well we may fall into conceit or pride; when there are difficulties or failures, we can fall into self-deprecation and depression.

How difficult it is to accept our limits and our handicaps as well as our gifts and capacities. We feel that if others see us as we really are they might reject us. So we cover over our weaknesses. I have experienced my own limits at certain moments, times when I realized there was great anger and violence rising up in me with respect to certain people with disabilities. Maybe it was because they seemed to be provoking me; maybe their anguish and feelings of loneliness called for my full attention at a time when I was not able to give it; maybe it was because I failed to alleviate their screams and their anguish. Or maybe it was deeper than all that: perhaps the anguish of those with intellectual disabilities awoke my own anguish, hidden in me since childhood.

Some people with disabilities call forth tenderness in me; others call forth anguish, fear, and anger. In a world of constant, and often quite intense, relationships, you quickly sense your inner limits, fears, and blockages. You can feel the anger rising up in you. When I was tired or preoccupied, my inner pain and anguish rose more quickly to the surface. In times of difficulty, it was hard to be open, welcoming, and patient. I have often come head-to-head with my own handicaps, limits, and inner poverty. I did not always find it easy, especially when my failure was evident to others.

But then I began to realize that in order to accept other people's disabilities and to help them to grow, it was fundamental for me to accept my own. I have, after all, learned something of my own character. I am gradually learning to accept my own shadow areas and to work with them in order to diminish their power over me.

The Road to Compassion

As I think back on my life, hidden in the secret recesses of my heart-memory, I discover or, perhaps, feel those who accepted and loved me just as I was. They did not judge me; there was unconditional love. One of those people who freed me to be more fully who I was and am was Father Thomas Philippe. I met him shortly after I had resigned from the navy in 1950. I lived with him and other seekers of truth and a meaningful life, in a small community he had founded just outside Paris. After years of separation, we met again in 1963, when he was the chaplain of an institution for men with intellectual disabilities. It was he who introduced me to people with intellectual disabilities and who helped me to see their value and importance in the world, for they are people of the heart. He encouraged me to begin l'Arche and he lived with us in the community almost to the time of his death.

Father Thomas was a man of heart. He loved people and he helped many to discover their true selves. As I experience Father Thomas today in my heart-memory, I feel the waters of forgiveness and goodness flowing from him, waters that refresh and help me regain trust in myself and in my secret name, that is to say, my mission in life, the reason I was born. Father Thomas was truly free and he, in turn, freed others.

To have an open heart that lets the waters of compassion, of understanding, and of forgiveness flow forth is a sign of a mature person. Maybe once in our lives we will be fortunate enough to meet such a person; we will feel cleansed, affirmed; we will discover our secret name. Then we, too, will walk towards greater freedom and let waters flow onto others, healing them and finding healing through them.

I am touched when I read the prophet Isaiah. He says that to please God is

> to break unjust chains
> to share your food with the hungry
> to shelter the homeless poor
> then you shall be like a watered garden,
> like a spring of water
> whose waters fail not   (Isaiah 58:6–7, 11)

The question we have to look at later is how to find this free and compassionate heart that opens up to those who are different. How can we move from a constricted, elitist concept of belonging, belonging which deprecates others, to this freedom of the heart that loves and appreciates those who are different?

Aung San Suu Kyi, the Buddhist who won the Nobel Peace Prize for her struggle for peace, human rights, and democracy in Burma, says,

All barriers of race and religion can be overcome when people work together in common endeavours, based on love and compassion. Together we can help to develop a happier, better world, where greed and ill-will and self-ishness are minimized. This is not impractical idealism; it is a down-to-earth recognition of our greatest needs.

Sometimes it takes courage to grapple with the difficulties that lie in the path of development. Unpopular decisions may have to be made and prejudices overcome. It may be necessary to defy despotic governments, to stand by the downtrodden and the underprivileged in the face of oppression and injustice. But "perfect love casts out fear," and everything becomes possible when charitable projects are carried out with true charity in the heart.[3]

In order to stand by the downtrodden, never to exclude but to include them in our lives, we need to be freed from our compulsive needs to succeed, to have power and approbation. We also need to be free from past hurts that govern our lives and cut us off from some people. We all need to grow to freedom. These are the subjects of the next two chapters.

I V

THE PATH
TO FREEDOM

IN THE PREVIOUS CHAPTER, I began by recounting the
parable that Jesus tells of Lazarus, the hungry beggar.
Lazarus spends his life looking with avid eyes at the
crumbs falling from the rich man's table, the table from
which he is excluded. By and by, the story goes, both
Lazarus and the rich man die and the rich man, from his
place of torment, can see Lazarus, blissfully happy in the
"heart of Abraham." The rich man begs that Lazarus be
allowed to bring him some water but he is reminded that
the abyss that separated them in life now separates them
in death.

I retell the story of Lazarus here because this chapter,
about the path to freedom, is in many ways a continuation
of the ideas I started to develop in the previous chapter.
Lazarus is a fitting image for us to focus on.

Exclusion generally refers to the way in which we
reject other human beings. It is something we do to entire
classes and groups, for example, those who are poor
or disabled. However, exclusion is also a very personal

matter. We are attracted to some people while we shun others. Those who attract us are often those who please us, help us, call us forth. If there is mutual attraction, there can be the beginning of a friendship. Those we shun, on the other hand, frighten us, maybe because we frighten them; we awaken feelings of rivalry and anguish in each other. And so, we create barriers that prevent openness. Maybe we feel that if we were open, we would lose something, that we would be hurt or swallowed up. We create barriers to protect our vulnerability.

We come together because we feel safe together. We encourage and support each other in the values we consider important and that give us life. But likes imply dislikes and fears. We are all more or less governed by our likes and dislikes — by the instincts and compulsions that lie deep within us. We are not totally free.

We understand the forces within us only imperfectly and we are not even entirely conscious of many of them. Animals have similar instincts. They can tell immediately if a smell, a sound, the movement of a bush, for example, is dangerous or not. We humans seem to have instincts that help us get out of difficult situations or to find what we need in order to go on living. Our brains interpret the most subtle of signals and trigger very fast reactions.

The ability to read subtle signs in the world around us is highly developed in humans. Why is this?

From a purely psychological point of view, we all want to feel good about ourselves and, so, we look for positive reinforcement from those around us. We need to be admired and appreciated; we need to feel loved and cared for. We need to feel that if we are absent, there is someone who will miss us. Just as instinctively as breathing, we flee those who make us feel helpless, inadequate, devalued, or anguished — all the things that make us feel bad about ourselves. This is a largely unconscious process but we can, of course, become conscious of these needs, just as we can become conscious of our breathing. We are quite deliberately selective of friends, for example, because we can read, in a more or less conscious way, how such a friendship will make us feel about ourselves and whether or not it will help us to advance in life and relieve us of the anguish of loneliness.

Freedom to Choose

We are more or less governed by instincts and drives that originate in the beautiful and painful experiences of childhood. We have little control over these drives; we are, nevertheless, more or less free as to the ways in which we might satisfy them.

What makes us feel good about ourselves varies greatly from person to person. For many of us, material success is very important; the classic goals are climbing the ladder of promotion, earning more money, gaining more honours, acquiring more privileges. For some, to be surrounded by a loving, happy family and friends is what they want. For others, success lies in being creative. Success can even mean being a good crook! A man in an American prison once told a friend of mine: "I'm the best car thief in Cleveland and I'm proud of it!" My friend was a priest, the prison chaplain, a man who was equally successful and admired in his own, very different, field as a priest and preacher.

To be a success, to be admired, means that we are competent in what we do. But for most of us, it's not enough just to be good at something. True success, we feel, comes from the recognition of others. This desire for success and admiration can be a good thing, for it encourages us to work well and hard; however, such a desire for success can draw us away from acting justly and serving others.

To be free is to put justice, truth, and service to others over and above our own personal gain or our need for recognition, power, honour, and success. When we cling to personal power and success, when we are frightened of losing social status, then we are in some way denying our humanity; we become slaves to our own needs. We are not free.

In 1944, in Marzobotto, a small town near Bologna in Italy, two thousand civilians were massacred by Nazi troops. The Nazis were retaliating for acts of sabotage committed by members of the Italian resistance. One young German soldier, however, refused to take part in the massacre and was shot.

That man was free, truly free. He put truth and justice above obedience to superiors and his desire to live at all costs. He refused to submit to evil.

History is filled with examples of free men and women who refused personal advancement, wealth, and power because they wanted to live in truth and in justice, according to their conscience, following ethical principles. We hear much about such men and women today in Algeria,

Rwanda, the former Zaire, Palestine, and in many other places, people who have taken sides with the poor and the oppressed, who have denounced injustice, cried out for freedom of speech, and who have been imprisoned, tortured, and killed.

Even in less extreme cases, there are many people who refuse material prosperity in order to live a life of service to those in need; they give generously of their time, energy, and knowledge so that others may eat, be clothed, find shelter, and live in peace.

We know, however, that the doer of good deeds can have a complex set of motivations. Underlying the act of generosity there can be a need for approval and, sometimes, even a need to exercise power, even spiritual power, over others.

These needs may provide the energy to orient one's life towards others, for the good of humanity, but at the same time they can tarnish our fundamental motivation, rendering it more or less self-serving. It is precisely such personal needs that must be purified so that acts of generosity may truly be for the inner growth and fulfillment of others, rather than for personal aggrandizement. To the degree that we no longer are governed by these needs, we will become free.

But how to embark on this road to freedom?

In the gospel there is a story of contrasting needs in two brothers. It is the story of the prodigal son. The younger of the two brothers asked his father for his part of the inheritance and then went off and squandered it all. Destitute and homesick, he decided to return home and ask his father for forgiveness. Maybe, he thought, his father would take him in, let him be a servant in the house.

The father, who was heartbroken at his son's departure, waited every day for his return. From far off he saw his son approaching and ran to meet him. Then the father called his servants and had them dress his son in fine clothes and threw a huge party to celebrate.

The elder son was furious. He shouted at his father: "You give a huge party for this good-for-nothing brother of mine, who wasted all your wealth, but you've never done anything like that for me." The father was unapologetic. He said, "my son who was lost has been found."

The younger son had felt compelled to leave his family; in today's language, we might say that he had wanted to find himself. His choice of what to do was unwise but he did take the risk of leaving, of living alone, and of searching out something new. The elder son, on the other hand, did something fairly conventional; he tried to please his father by staying home.

I suspect, though, that neither of these sons really knew their father. The younger son never imagined that he could be loved just as he was, although his father gave him the freedom to be himself. The elder son did not realize, either, that by staying at home he was called on by his father to love and be compassionate.

The two attitudes of this man's sons are in many of us. There are those who want to be free spirits and risk new ways. There are also those who have a greater need to fit in, to meet the norm.

The younger son broke away from his father to find his

identity; the elder son sought to conform. Both of these men were driven, like most of us, by forces that they understood imperfectly. What is important is that each of us gradually becomes aware of the things that drive us, that we freely choose our path and affirm what we believe, not out of a sense of rebellion or of a need to conform, but in order to serve a larger vision of life, to work for justice, and to help people stand up in truth.

The varieties of our fears, anxieties, and desires lead us to behaviour that we don't understand very well; we can be driven by strong forces that push towards security, tranquility, and conventional success; the same forces make us flee all that we fear: rejection, feelings of helplessness and inadequacy, conflict. To become truly free is to give more importance to truth and justice than to the desire to fulfill at all costs our own compulsive needs. It's a paradox, though. These needs are part of our being; we need them in order to advance in life but we also need to learn how to govern them rather than be governed by them.

We can get so focused on a particular goal that we leave other parts of our being underdeveloped. That is what happened to me. To some people, the total commitment I had to my profession as a naval officer was something laudable and I'm sure it was. But at the same time, this commitment was impoverishing me because I left other parts of my being — my heart, my intelligence — undeveloped.

Compulsions, I think, affect all of us. Some people have a compulsive need to help others, to do things for them, sometimes in the name of God and of justice. They go on

and on, living a life full of doing in return for an affection-
ate response, but such people are frequently unable to
take time to look after themselves. They burn out. What is
most beautiful in them can become what is worst. Their
generosity becomes their downfall, because it flows
more from a need to feel wanted and loved than from a
true desire for others to be well and free.

In order to help other people, we have to understand
their needs. Can we do that if we are unaware of our own
needs? When we help other people isn't it so that they
become free, no longer dependent on us?

Some people have a compulsive need to maintain power
and control over others. They are terribly insecure and
can be frightened of the freedom of others. What might
happen if they lose control? They may be knowledgeable,
they may teach and guide others, but their need for power
and control, and sometimes spiritual power in order to do
"the things of God," makes them unfree. It leads them
away from true love and the gift of self. Knowledge and
power become their downfall.

Other people, because of their insecurity, feel a compulsive need to belong. They seek approval from others.
Belonging becomes the place where they can hide. They
conform and are frightened of revealing who they really
are; they do not allow the deepest part of themselves to
rise up. They are unable to be creative; they tend to be
legalistic. They can use religion and ethics to feel superior.
They need to be seen as good, worthy, obedient, and
holy. Religion and ethical values are no longer there to
help them to be open to others and to risk loving but

to reinforce a positive image of themselves, a feeling of superiority, of being part of an elite.

Behind Compulsive Needs: Anguish

The compulsive need to succeed, to do things for others, to be better than others, can also become addictive. Addictions keep urging you forward. Over the years, they take up all your energy; nothing else attracts or interests you. In effect, they come to make up your character and what I call your "false self." When these compulsive needs are not met, a void appears; it is a feeling, literally, of dis-ease or of anguish; you feel lost or confused, as if you have lost the knowledge of who you are. And like the more familiar reformed addict, the one who has been cut off from drugs, it takes time for new interests and desires to appear, for the void to be filled, and for a new identity to be created.

We have compulsive needs: to win, to control, to be loved. Likewise, we have compulsive fears: inner blockages, fears of some relationships, of conflict. These compulsions push us forward but they also constrain us. They close us in on ourselves, make us blind to our own limits and brokenness, and to the beauty and gifts of those who are different. Under the control of our compulsions, others can quickly become a threat: they stand in the way of the love or success we seem to need so badly.

Jesus was an astute psychologist. He said: "Do not try to take the speck of dust out of someone's eye when you have a log in your own! Take out the log from your own eye, then you will be able to see more clearly in order to take out the speck of dust in the eye of the other" (Matthew 7:3).

It is so easy to judge others and to see their faults and limits. How difficult it is to see our own! When we do, they can depress us. So, we either think we are wonderful, at the centre of the universe, or horrible, in the garbage dump of humanity. It is almost impossible, humanly speaking, to be aware of our limits, our faults and weaknesses, to accept them, and then to grow to become more compassionate.

Compassion is maturity and maturity is acceptance. Maturity is precisely the acceptance of yourself with your own flaws, as well as others with their flaws.

Maturity, then, is to discover who we are. Socrates said, "Know thyself." That remains a fundamental need. As we begin to know ourselves, with our gifts and flaws, our yearnings for truth and justice, and our compulsions and blockages, we begin to take our places in society, each of us just as we are, working for peace, unity, and justice. But now we do this in a more holistic way.

We need some guidelines about what to accept and strengthen in ourselves and what to change or redirect. Perhaps we all have such guidelines that are difficult to articulate and that we cannot prove because they are fundamental; they belong to the category of first principles. To me, for example, life is a first principle: I believe in the sacredness of every human being and that each one is called to be fully alive.

We can find fulfillment only if we all work together to create a society where each of us is moving from narcissistic and egocentric tendencies, where we are closed up in self, to a state of openness towards others; we can find fulfillment only in working together to find a greater fullness to humanity. It is the truthful acceptance of self, and the desire to live in truth, in justice, and in love, that is the basis of freedom.

Our patterns of behaviour are neither good nor bad, in themselves, but they can become burdensome and unhealthy. In order to grow humanly we have to recognize them in ourselves and make choices about their appropriateness.

Aristotle talks of our passions as being like a horse which has a life of its own. We are riders who have to take into account the life of the horse in order to guide it where we want it to go. We are not called to suppress our passions or compulsions, nor to confront them head on, nor to be governed by them, but to orientate them in the direction we want to go. In this way, we may find the fulfillment of our own humanity, and work, according to our gifts, for the fulfillment of the humanity of others.

We set out on the road to freedom when we no longer let our compulsions or passions govern us. We are freed when we begin to put justice, heartfelt relationships, and the service of others and of truth over and above our own needs for love and success or our fears of failure and of relationships.

The road to freedom is never easy; it involves a real struggle. Inner pain and feelings of distress emerge as we change and try to live in greater truth and emerge from our self-centredness. When we free ourselves from our compulsions, we can suffer symptoms of grief and feelings of inner emptiness.

Signs of Freedom

What is this freedom? Read part of this poem by Rudyard
Kipling. It is called "If."

> If you can keep your head when all about you
> are losing theirs and blaming you,
> If you can trust yourself when all men doubt you,
> But make allowance for their doubting too;
> If you can wait and not be tired of waiting,
> or being lied about, don't deal in lies,
> or being hated, don't give way to hating . . .[4]

Freedom is the freedom of truth. Jesus said, "The truth
will set you free." A lack of freedom equals fear — fear of
reality, fear of others; lack of freedom means clinging to
illusions and prejudices and sometimes even to lies. A
lack of freedom means being governed by compulsions
instead of governing them. It is imposing a vision on
reality or wanting to change reality through force instead
of forming a new vision of reality. Lack of freedom means
thinking that you alone have the truth and that others are
wrong or stupid. It means being controlled by prejudice.

In the previous chapter, I talked about people's fear of
those with intellectual disabilities and about the many
prejudices against them. Frequently, these fears are
groundless. Some of those who are frightened of people
with intellectual disabilities may never have met anyone
with disabilities. When they get to know them, however,
their fears and prejudices usually dissipate. On the other
hand, for some people, their fears and prejudices are so

deeply rooted that they refuse to meet any person who has a disability. They already "know" that those with disabilities are "mad" and useless. Prejudices like these are frequently based on a great fear of change; people do not want to be disturbed in their security or have their value systems questioned. They do not want to open their hearts to those who are different. People with prejudices are not free.

To be free is to know who we are, with all that is beautiful, all the brokenness in us; it is to love our own values, to embrace them, and to develop them; it is to be anchored in a vision and a truth but also to be open to others and, so, to change. Freedom lies in discovering that the truth is not a set of fixed certitudes but a mystery we enter into, one step at a time. It is a process of going deeper and deeper into an unfathomable reality.

In this journey of integrating our experience and our values, and of what we might learn as we listen to others, there may be a period of anguish. We need to find links between the old and the new, links that will permit the integration of new, consciousness-expanding truths into what we already know and are living — our existing certitudes. As human sciences develop and the world evolves, we are called to grow into a new and deeper understanding of the Source of the universe and of life. As we participate in this, our sense of the true expands. Freedom is to be in awe of this Source, of the beauty and diversity of people, and of the universe. It is to contemplate the height and breadth of all that is true.

Freedom is to accept that when we belong to a group, a

race, a tribe, a family, a community, a religion, that none
of these is perfect, that each has its limits and weaknesses.
Every community of humans has its light and its darkness. We are all part of something greater than ourselves.
We all flow from a source that is unfathomable and we are
all journeying towards it, carrying with us the light of
truth and love. Each of us is called to be in communion
with the source and heart of the universe. The infinite
yearnings of our hearts are calling us to be in communion
with the Infinite. None of us can be satisfied with the
limited and the finite. Each one must be free to follow
the Spirit of God.

And this freedom is for love and compassion, to give our
lives more totally and more freely to others. It is the
freedom to be kind and patient. This freedom does not
seek personal honours; it believes all, hopes all, bears
all, and endures all. Freedom does not judge or condemn
but understands and forgives. Freedom is the liberation
from all those inner fears that make us hide from people
and from reality. It is also the humble acceptance of the
fact that we do have fears and inhibitions and that we need
to ask forgiveness of those we have hurt.

There is a freedom that I sense exists but that I do not
have. I cannot always describe it but I do want it. I sense I
still have a long road to walk in order to reach this freedom. I see the goal but I am not yet there. I love and want
it but sometimes I am frightened of the road I must take.

I am frightened of the disappearance of my walls of
defence, sensing that behind them there is an anguish and
a vulnerability that will rise up. I see that I still cling to

what people think of me and am fed by the way people love, want, and admire me. If all that fell away, who would I be? But that is where freedom lies, the freedom to be rejected, if that is the path I am to take in order to live more fully. Is that not the freedom that Jesus announces in his charter of the Beatitudes, when he talks of the blessedness of those who are persecuted, or when he says, "Woe to you when people speak well of you"?

I suppose in my own way, but in a very different context, I can relate to Nelson Mandela's words:

I am not truly free if I am taking away someone else's freedom, just as surely as I am not free when my freedom is taken from me . . . to be free is not merely to cast off one's chains, but to live in a way that respects and enhances the freedom of others.

And he goes on:

I have walked that long road to freedom. I have tried not to falter; I have made missteps along the way. But I have discovered the secret that after climbing a great hill, one only finds that there are many more hills to climb. I have taken a moment here to rest, to steal a view of the glorious vista that surrounds me, to look back on the distance I have come. But I can rest only for a moment, for with freedom comes responsibilities, and I dare not linger; for my long walk is not yet ended.[5]

My main teacher on the road to freedom is Jesus, and I am thankful to my church, which has brought me closer to Him. I am touched and attracted by His total freedom and yearn to find that. It is the freedom the apostle Paul speaks of:

> Above all brothers and sisters you are called to be free;
> Do not use your freedom for an openness to self-indulgence,
> but be servants to one another in love. . . .
> The fruit of the Spirit is love, joy, peace, patience,
> kindness, truthfulness, gentleness and self-control.
> No law can touch such things as these.
>
> (Galatians 5:13, 22–23)

Freedom Is Also the Death of the False Self

In one of his last books, the historian and ecumenical theologian Donald Nicholl speaks of the liberation that comes from the death of the false "I" — the ego.

> Japanese Buddhists speak of two "I's": one of them is the "I" that is susceptible to study by psychology, [and that] strives to satisfy its desires, talks about itself, observes its reactions, displays itself, and is eminently visible. It is known as *shoga* and has to perish if the other "I" is to be properly born. This latter, known as *taiga*, refers to the whole human being when that whole human being is entirely taken up in an aspiration and prayer.

Nicholl compares this second "I" to what the "Song of Songs" speaks of: "I sleep (or the ego has gone to sleep)," he says, "but my heart is awake" (Song of Solomon 5:2). He explains that "if the heart is not to be hindered in its deepest aspirations, then the ego, that partial self, which is always watching itself and composing a role for it to play, must disappear."[6]

Donald Nicholl touches on a great truth. Don't all spiritual masters speak of the dying of self in order for the real self to emerge? The false self they refer to is not just the visible passions, but all those hidden compulsions that push us to seek our own glory. When Jesus talked about the liberation of love, he said, "Truly, truly, I say to you, unless the grain of wheat falls into the ground and dies, it remains alone; but if it dies, it bears much fruit. Whoever loves their life, loses it; whoever hates their life in this world, will keep it for eternal life" (John 12:24–25). The "life" is that of the false ego, and the "eternal life" is not life after death, but the life that we are called to live in the freedom of love.

The death of the false self, the ego, is more painful in people who have created a strong, imposing, and dominating self. Its death is less painful in those who are weaker or who have never sought to have power, though it can be painful for those who lack trust in themselves.

This freedom that comes through the death of the false self is the acceptance of ourselves just as we are. It is also the acceptance of the world as it is together with the will to struggle to make the world a better place for us to live. This freedom means we do not weep for the past and long to walk backwards. It is not to shout out against the decadence or chaos of our times, nor to close ourselves off in sectarian groups, filled with fear. It is not to cry out "Tragedy, the end of the world has come!" or to be paralyzed by today's injustices. Nor is it to believe naively that at last humanity is being liberated, and that all will be well. To be free is to see new truths emerging in the chaos, to see the Spirit of God hovering over the chaos. It is to see the emergence of new and positive realities from behind the certitudes and prejudices of yesterday.

Every age, every generation, is confronted by new realities, new tragedies, new difficulties, but also new truths. The world and our human societies in it are evolving; every day, new things are being revealed. We live in an exciting age. There are numerous new technologies that can ruin the planet and deep fears that close people and communities up in themselves. In spite of, or perhaps because of, all the fears, evil, lies, and hatred in and around us, we must strive to discern what the Spirit of God is calling for us to be and do.

The Spirit of God is constantly revealing new things for our age, even a new spirituality. In Christian churches there is a desire to rediscover the essential message of love and forgiveness rather than to be caught up in legalities, rituals, and the debate about who is right and who is wrong. Many people of different religions have the common desire to meet, to share, to enter into a dialogue, and to pray. This desire for unity is not necessarily widespread, but it *is* there in the hearts of many all over the world. It is a seed that will grow and bear much fruit.

Each one of us has a responsibility to work towards the liberation of all people. There are new things in store for us all. Let us be open to welcome them. We are called to discern where the truth lies today.

The Road to Freedom

Is this a utopian vision, an impossible ideal? Can we really walk to freedom, or are our egos' needs simply too great? Are we hardwired to put ourselves at the centre and do everything for our own glory? Are we too frightened of letting our true selves emerge? Can we break out of our individual and collective selfishness and need for security to work for peace and the common good of humankind? Can we reasonably have a dream, like Martin Luther King, of a world where people, whatever their race, religion, culture, abilities, or disabilities, whatever their education or economic situation, whatever their age or gender, can find a place and reveal their gifts? Can we hope for a society whose metaphor is not a pyramid but a body, and where each of us is a vital part in the harmony and function of the whole?

I believe we can, because I believe that the aspiration for peace, communion, and universal love is greater and deeper in people than the need to win in the competition of life. But for this aspiration to become a real desire that inspires our activities, in order for it to break through our fears and the need to win, each one of us has to make a leap into trust: trust in the sacredness of every human heart, trust in the beauty of the universe, trust that in working for peace and unity, and in purging our false self, we will find a treasure.

But an inspiration or a call to trust comes often in a moment of grace, in a gentle ray of light, in a moment of awareness of who we really are. Then we must walk forward and strengthen this inspiration by making clear choices and a commitment.

We must not be naive, however. There are immense forces that break down trust: evil, hatred, and lies do exist; there *are* people who seek to oppress, to destroy, and to kill. We all need to be helped to discern clearly where there is life and truth and where there is illusion and death.

As I have already said, this freedom is not for an elite. For most people, like myself, it is something for which we have to work and struggle. It is a long but beautiful road. Some people seem to have fewer barriers, fewer defence mechanisms; their compulsions seem to be weaker. I have met wonderful mothers who seem whole and integrated. I have met wise and gentle men and women who are open and free. I have met people with disabilities who have an astounding freedom; they do not seem to be imprisoned in prejudice. I have met people with mental illness who are free in their hearts; they know they are ill, but they have understood and accepted their limits. I have met many people in slum areas and in broken situations all over the world who seem wonderfully free, uncluttered by the need for power and human glory.

I am in awe of such people, and I love and admire them. There is a presence of God in them, a gentleness, a compassion, a wholeness, and a humility. Their hearts are open to others, and perhaps that is why they are so vulnerable, fragile, and easily hurt. And if they do not protect themselves, is it not because they know they are held in the arms of God? This freedom is for all. Some are closer to it. Others among us have to work harder for it, because we have stronger defences to overcome.

The steps to freedom that I outline here are for all of us who must struggle along the path.

The first step to freedom is to learn that fear can be a good counsellor. Strange as it may seem, an experience of fear can lead us to yearn for freedom. It can turn us around and make us reflect and change course. Fear is provoked by a crisis and calls us together to talk, reflect, ask questions, and seek solutions. Drastic situations, such as in Northern Ireland, the civil war in Guatemala, or the genocide in Bosnia and Rwanda, can oblige people from all sides to stop and ask the question: Do we really want peace? More generic causes of suffering, such as the international armaments industry and the multinational companies that dominate the global economy, make us ask: Do we want a world built on the principle of competition, where the strong win by killing and oppressing? Do we want to be governed solely by economics? Can the panther and the baby goat lie down together, as in Isaiah's prophecy? Is it possible to work for peace and love?

The second step to freedom involves becoming aware of our own limits and blockages. It took time for me to become aware of my own limits. While in the navy in the early 1950s, at the height of the Cold War, I knew we were on the "right side," that the communists were bad. We had to be prepared to fight for peace. After that, when I studied philosophy and theology, I learned what was true and what was false. I learned about the errors in different philosophical and political systems and the theological errors in other religious traditions.

Perhaps at some point in our lives we all need to believe

in an ideal, even an ideology, where the line between good and bad, and true and false, is clearly drawn. At these moments we see ourselves as part of an elite, with all the truth, saving the world from chaos and evil. Perhaps we all have to embrace the strong beliefs of adolescence before we can become mature adults with the wisdom to modify our certitudes and listen respectfully to those who bring us different views.

It took time for me to see and accept the brokenness in the history and life of my own church, and to discover the beauty, truth, and good in other churches and religions. Just as it took time for me to discover all that was broken in myself: my prejudices, my fears, my mixed motivations, my weaknesses, my need to succeed, and my fear of failure.

Spiritual masters in different religions teach that there are steps in the growth to freedom. Buddhism teaches that there are four different "heavenly abodes," or divine states of mind. The first, *metta*, is loving kindness, a love that seeks to give and serve rather than to take and demand. The second, *keruna*, is compassion, a quivering heart in response to another's suffering, the wish to remove that which is painful from the lives of others. The third, *mudita*, is sympathetic joy, a joyfulness in the heart as we perceive the weak, the poor, and the oppressed rising up in freedom. The fourth, *pekka*, is a peace of heart that is beyond the attainment of ordinary human beings, with the ordinary capacity for controlling our minds and emotions.

Christian spiritual writers also speak of the steps to freedom. At first there is the struggle against the powerful but superficial passions of greed and pleasure, and against selfishness and blatant self-centredness, in order to live a life governed by truth, service, and prayer.

This struggle is facilitated by entering into a place of belonging. There we can continue our intellectual and spiritual formation with brothers and sisters and so conquer more easily our superficial passions. More subtle passions arise, however: feelings of intellectual and spiritual superiority, disdain for those outside, the need to control others. But the struggle continues as we see we must die to our false self, the spiritual ego, in order to become one with God in poverty, freedom, littleness, and humility, loving others as God loves them.

I, too, had to grow out of established beliefs and certitudes towards maturity and wisdom. I had to look at my own brokenness, hidden by my unconscious need to be a "spiritual success." Even now, at the age of seventy, my desire to be free is growing. It is never too late!

Is it possible for us to grow to greater freedom if we are not conscious of our lack of freedom? Can we yearn to see if we do not realize we are blind? Where do we find the hope, the energy, and the desire to work towards that freedom and new sight? All spiritual writers speak of the pain and brokenness we experience as we move from the security of certitudes through uncertainty to wisdom. Wisdom implies a certain poverty in the heart and spirit. It is this inner poverty and humility that opens the heart to a new joy, a new freedom, a new meeting with God.

The third step to freedom is to look for the wisdom that comes from unexpected events: the death of a friend, sickness, an accident that creates a severe disability, or an apparent misfortune that breaks the pattern of our life and obliges us to reevaluate our lives, to find new values.

Such events come as surprises that open us up to the new and the universal. They appear to be tragic because they move us from the secure world of the predictable to the chaotic world of the unexpected, and thus into anguish. But later we can discover that they are blessed events. Many times parents of people with disabilities have told me about the shock they received at the birth of their child. Then they discovered that their child was leading them from a world of power and competition into a world of tenderness and compassion. Crises and unexpected changes can lead us to denial, despair, anger, and revolt, but these feelings can gradually help us to accept reality as it is and discover in the new situation new energies, a new freedom, and a new meaning of life and of the world.

For this discovery, people often need help from somebody who "walks with them," an accompanier. One of the most important factors for inner liberation is how we are accompanied. We must ask ourselves: Who is walking with me?

So my fourth step to freedom involves accompaniment. An accompanier is someone who can stand beside us on the road to freedom, someone who loves us and understands our life. An accompanier can be a parent, a teacher, or a friend — anyone who can put a name on our inner pain and feelings. Accompaniers may be professionals or therapists, those who have experience in untying the knots that block us in our development. They may be ordained ministers or other people who have grown in the ways of God, who seek to help us understand each other's humanity and needs, and who help us recognize God's call to communion, inner liberation, and a greater love of self.

Accompaniment is necessary at every stage of our lives, but particularly in moments of crisis when we feel lost, engulfed in grief or in feelings of inadequacy. The accompanier is there to give support, to reassure, to confirm, and to open new doors. The accompanier is not there to judge us or to tell us what to do, but to reveal what is most beautiful and valuable in us, as well as to point towards the meaning of our inner pain. In this way, an accompanier helps us advance to greater freedom by helping us to be reconciled to our past and to accept ourselves as we are, with our gifts and our limits.

I was fortunate to meet Father Thomas Philippe when I left the navy. He was my accompanier for many years. He was always there when I needed him, especially when I began l'Arche. He never judged me but always accepted me and brought out the best in me. Because I was well accompanied, I was able to open up my heart. I did not keep things hidden within, where they could rot and decay. I was able to name my weaknesses and fears.

The word "accompaniment," like the word "companion," comes from the Latin words *cum pane*, which mean "with bread." It implies sharing together, eating together, nourishing each other, walking together. The one who accompanies is like a midwife, helping us to come to life, to live more fully. But the accompanier receives life also, and as people open up to each other, a communion of hearts develops between them. They do not clutch on to each other but give life to one another and call each other to greater freedom.

So it was easy for me, in turn, to accompany other people, to trust in them, to remove some of the guilt that weighed on their shoulders, and to help them discover their value.

Accompaniment is at the heart of community life in l'Arche, but it is at the heart of all human growth. We human beings need to walk together, encouraging each other to continue the journey of growth and the struggle for liberation, and to break through the shell of egotism that engulfs us and prevents us from realizing our full humanity.

My fifth step to freedom has to do with role models — people who are witnesses to truth and have a clear vision. Each of us on our road can see that others before us have walked the same road to freedom. Over the last century, there have been a number of great, free figures: Mahatma Gandhi, the Dalai Lama, Mother Teresa. We can each make our own list of those who, maybe in a hidden, quiet way, are freely giving of their lives so that others might have a better life and find hope. There are men and women who struggle to bring food and help to the needy, and peace where there is conflict. There are many men and women who have struggled to make our world more habitable. They have lived what they preached; they have given of their lives for truth and love.

A model is someone who demonstrates new ways of living in spite of all the chaos, someone who remains loving and humble in spite of all the violence, someone who does not judge or condemn. Through their lives, these people show us a bigger picture: that there is a way to peace and unity, even though it may involve struggle and pain.

The sixth step is to recognize that the road to freedom is also a struggle. It is hard work to liberate oneself from inner compulsions, to commit oneself to inner growth, truth, justice, and the service of others. This struggle means many things. It means making an effort not to speak of others from the place of our inner wounds and fears, thus devaluing and judging them. It means not avoiding those who are different, but rather approaching them with a listening heart. For some, it means visiting places where those who are different are gathered together: prisons, psychiatric wards, institutions for people with disabilities, slums, foreign lands. It means taking time to listen to individuals — their pains, their hopes, their anger, and their depression. This is a constant struggle, something we will always do imperfectly.

This struggle can become more simple as we get older. Wisdom often comes with age, as long as we accept to fully live our old age. We no longer have to be in command or be quick and efficient; we do not need to have an important place in society. We finally have time to be, to enjoy nature, to do things we never had time to do before. We no longer have to prove ourselves. We have more time to be with people in heartfelt relationships, to pray, and to rest in communion with God. Is this not the true meaning of old age, which our modern societies tend to devalue? If, as old people, we do not seek to live this wisdom, isn't there a danger that we will fall into depression, because we have lost our energy, roles, and sometimes health, but have not discovered what we have gained?

The seventh step on the road to freedom is the recognition that the liberation of the heart comes about when we live in communion with the Source of the universe, with God. God touches us in the core of our being, deeper than our compulsions for power and admiration or our fears of rejection and feelings of guilt. God reveals the uniqueness and preciousness of our being just as we are.

Throughout the history of humankind, mystics have sought to liberate themselves from their ego, their fundamental selfishness, in order to live in a deeper union with God and to be free to love as God loves — with compassion. There have also been men and women who, though they may not have specifically sought a union with God, were seekers of truth and compassion, and worked for peace and the unity of humanity.

This union with God, this trust that we are loved by God and held in the arms of God, gives us inner strength and fortifies our desire *to be*, and *to be true*. It permits us to see each person, each event, the great march of history, and the whole universe itself as God sees them. This in itself diminishes our need to prove ourselves or to hide behind barriers of power or knowledge. It lessens our fears of being rejected. It also prevents us from making an absolute of anything. No one person, no one group, not even humanity in its entirety is God.

This communion with God does not create a tension between our bodies and our spirit. God is at the source of all our being — spirit and matter. This communion brings us to inner wholeness. The danger for us is to block off the life that flows into us from the heart and Source of the universe when we seek affirmation of our ego in a constant search for power and recognition. With the death of our false self, we liberate the life of God in us and, in the words of Martin Buber, we allow God to flow through our hearts and our beings and thus to enter into our world.

The message of Jesus has often been mangled. Yet Jesus came to lead us all into a society that is a *body*, where each part, weak or strong, able or disabled, finds its place and is free. This vision for humanity, which is a vision of goodness and compassion for each person, comes from a God of Love, who wants to change our hearts of stone into hearts of flesh.

Humanity needs to return to this humble, loving God who is all heart. It needs to rediscover the message of gentleness, tenderness, nonviolence, and forgiveness, to rediscover the beauty of our universe, of matter, of our own bodies, and of all life. This path of rediscovery will be a struggle, but a worthwhile one.

This message of love brings with it a secret, gentle ecstasy of love, a new peace of heart, an inner liberation. It is not just for the strong-willed and the austere, but for all those who open their hearts to this God of Love. The inner liberation is for those whose true self is hidden behind high walls, for those whose character and personality have been built on fear but who trust in the liberating force of

God's love. It is for all those who are locked up in prisons of past hurts and who are discovering little by little the road to forgiveness.

And this is the subject for my last chapter: forgiveness. This is the ultimate secret of liberation: to forgive and to be forgiven, and thus to become free, like little children.

V

FORGIVENESS

THE GREEK WORD for forgiveness is *asphesis*, which means to liberate, to release from bondage; it means the remission of debt, guilt, and punishment. It is used when the prison door is opened and the prisoner can go free.

We humans are called to become free, to free others, to nurture life, to look for the worth and the beauty in each and every one of us, and to make of our world a beautiful garden where each person and each society can create a harvest of flowers and fruits, and so prepare the seeds of peace for tomorrow.

In the last chapter, I talked about becoming free of the inner compulsions towards success, the drive to be admired, and the fear of rejection. When these compulsions and cravings govern our behaviour and prevent us from seeking justice and freedom for others, we are not free. In this chapter, I want to talk about finding freedom from those inner hurts that govern our behaviour and make us act inhumanly towards others.

Some of these hurts have been actively inflicted on us,

for example, through verbal or physical abuse. Other wounds come more passively: at certain times, particularly when we were weak and in need, we have felt unappreciated and rejected. In either case, our needs were ignored by those who might have helped but who passed us by. Our hurts leave wounds in the heart, pushed down and covered over in the recesses of our being. These hurts are at the origin of the barriers that we create.

These barriers and the wounds they cover up prevent healthy belonging because they prevent communication and openness. In order to become truly free, which is to be most human, these barriers have to be removed. Forgiveness is this process of removing barriers; it is the process by which we start to accept and to love those who have hurt us. This is the final stage of inner liberation.

We react to hurts in different ways. We can be driven to hurt those who have hurt us, to speak evil of those who have spoken evil of us. There are other ways of dealing with hurts. Some of us let the hurt fester inside, creating an attitude of continual dis-ease and discontent with everything and everyone. The hurt that we hide can even turn into feelings of self-deprecation, as if we deserved it, because we have become convinced that we have no value.

Hurts can also create feelings of guilt. There are two types of guilt: psychological guilt and moral guilt. The first is induced in us by others, those who have made us feel that we are without value. Psychologists frequently call this first type of guilt "shame" in order to distinguish it from the second type, the one we induce in ourselves after having done something we consider wrong. Psychological guilt is not the consequence of having hurt someone or of committing a crime; it is the feeling that can overwhelm us when we feel rejected as individuals.

Many years ago John Paul came to l'Arche from a psychiatric hospital. At one point he became quite mentally ill and started to have hallucinations. He moved out of reality and began to live in another world, a situation that was frightening for him as well as for the rest of us. All those who were involved with his care had a meeting with Erol Franko, our psychiatrist at the time. We wanted to understand what had provoked the crisis and how to help John Paul find himself again and rediscover reality. I still remember Dr. Franko's words: "I believe John Paul feels guilty for existing." He reminded us that, because of his disability, this young man had been rejected by his parents, then by his grandparents, and yet again by two family placements. He eventually ended up in a psychiatric hospital before coming to l'Arche. Never in his life had he felt accepted or loved just as he was. He had never felt bonded to anyone. He had always been seen as a nuisance and a disturbance. If we are not loved, then we feel unlovable. This is psychological guilt, which touches us to our core.

Moral guilt and psychological guilt feed into each other. If we feel that we have no worth, it is because we have been told, in one way or another, that this is so. We will then act accordingly: we will hurt others precisely because we know we have no worth and can only do worthless things.

Many of the people with intellectual disabilities come to l'Arche filled with this psychological guilt. They are convinced that they are no good, and that they can do no good. The purpose of the l'Arche communities is to help people move from their broken, negative self-image into a positive one. We try to help them move from a desire to die to a desire to live, from self-hatred to self-love.

These feelings of worthlessness are induced in all of us as children whenever we feel rejected. Thus in childhood the shadow side of our being develops within us, and these feelings surface during moments of depression. To be depressed is to be flooded by feelings that paralyze us and prevent us from getting on with our lives. This psychological guilt is also at the root of our lack of trust in ourselves. Many of us lack trust not just in our ability to do something that demands experience and competence, but in our capacity to love, and to be loved in return.

As I listen to people I discover how many of us are weighed down by guilt. Mothers and fathers feel guilty because they are imperfect parents. Husbands and wives feel guilty because they do not know how to love and care for their partner. Perhaps we all feel guilty because we are not quite who we wanted to become; to that extent all of us are disappointed in ourselves so we disappoint others. The question, then, is how to free ourselves from the weight of guilt? How can we rediscover the trust and faith that helps us to open up to others and do something beautiful with our lives? How can mother and child, or husband and wife, liberate one another from the feelings that prevent them from living fully? How can there be an encounter between them that releases a new energy, transforming their hearts? This is the energy the Jewish philosopher Martin Buber refers to in his book *I and Thou* when he speaks of two people who truly meet together and reveal themselves to each other.

In the first chapter, I spoke about the love that transforms people, and that transformed Claudia, a young woman with severe disabilities in the l'Arche community in Honduras. This love reveals, understands, empowers, celebrates, and helps people move from the desire to die to the desire to live. This love liberates us from the tentacles of psychological guilt which paralyzes us. It is a love that flows from someone who believes in us and wants us to live. But we have to open our hearts to receive this love. We can block it, refuse to believe in it, or not want it at all. Sometimes the desire to die can be overwhelming.

Here, I think, is the secret of our inner freedom. We can either welcome or refuse this transforming love. To for*give* is to offer this love that liberates people from the powers of moral and psychological guilt. It is the supreme *gift*, the greatest of gifts, because it is a gift of liberation from all the hurts of the past, hurts that prevent us from living fully and loving others.

Personal Hurts

Let us look at different types of hurt. First, there are personal hurts: one individual making another suffer.

A young university student came to see me. From the way she spoke about men I sensed a lot of pain in her. I asked her to tell me about her relationship with her father.

She glared at me: "I hate him!" I wanted to know more.
She told me that her father was a philosophy teacher in a
Christian school and was greatly loved and respected.
When he came home, however, he locked himself up in his
room. "He never eats with us," she said. "He never speaks
to me. I hate him."

It is not easy for a young woman to feel rejected and
slighted by a father who should encourage and confirm
her. Her father made her feel she was worthless. His
rejection fed into her general sense of rejection and created
deep tension, anger, and revolt in her. It was also affecting
all her relationships with men. This young woman needed
to be liberated from the hatred that was governing her life.
It was important for her to start understanding her father,
a process that might eventually lead to forgiveness.

When she begins to understand her father and why he
acts in that way, she will be on the road to forgiveness.
But this forgiveness can only become a true meeting and
communion of hearts if her father is willing to reflect on
his behaviour, if he realizes how much he has hurt his
daughter, and asks her for this gift of forgiveness. Only
then could reconciliation, total healing, and liberation
take place in both.

Sometimes the essential issue is not understanding, but
recognizing that there are blockages in the one who has
hurt us that can lead to a refusal to admit guilt. A young
woman had been in prison for a number of years because
of a man who gave false evidence against her. In prison,
she experienced a spiritual transformation through the
help of the prison chaplain. One day, the chaplain brought

up the issue of forgiving this man who had brought so much hardship on her. "No," she replied, "I could never forgive him; he has hurt me too much. But I pray each day that God may forgive him."

This woman seemingly could not forgive until her persecutor fully repented and asked for the gift of forgiveness. But she also showed that she did not want to be controlled by her hatred for him. Even more, she wanted him to live in truth; she prayed for him. In some cases, it is easier for the victim to move towards this inner liberation than for the oppressor to admit guilt and ask for forgiveness. In other cases, the hurt can be so deep in the victim that complete liberation is a very long and painful process. Think of the Jews who survived the extermination camps, or the Tutsis and Hutus who have lived through the massacres in Rwanda.

Imprisoned in One's Likes and Dislikes

Most of us don't have to deal with the kind of hatred the university student and the woman in jail felt, but we all have sharp likes and dislikes. We discover these as we live with others in family, at work, in a community, or in other groups. We are attracted to some people and we reject others. We hand out praise and condemnation with equal ease. And even if we do not praise or condemn, we do place people in easy categories. Those who belong to another church or political party, or who profess other values are quickly given a label. Those who belong to a different race or social class are assigned a place in the order of the world as we see it. We like to see ourselves at the top of a pyramid; we look down on those who are different; we do not see them as our brothers and sisters. We may not always hate others, but we are very quick to categorize them. As humans, we put up barriers with ease.

But not all of our dislikes about people are groundless. There are those who belittle us. There are others who awaken latent fears. Still others make us feel anxious and uneasy. Some people want to possess us, so we feel constrained in their presence. Others appear as rivals in some domain or another. All of these various dislikes have one thing in common: they spring from the perception of danger to our sense of self.

Likes and dislikes are motivated by our own natural needs and fears. We are attracted to those who seem to affirm and encourage us, who love and admire us. We reject those who do not affirm or encourage us but who judge and condemn. We may not be imprisoned in anything as strong as hate, but our likes and dislikes create equally high walls of prejudice. Behind them we can act as if others do not exist, or as if they do not belong to our common humanity.

To be truly liberated, we have to make an effort to communicate with those we dislike, to try to understand and accept them as they are, and to experience our mutual humanity. This is forgiveness.

Hatred of a Group of People

Then there are the hatreds that communities generate in each other.

In *My First White Friend: Confessions on Race, Love and Forgiveness*, the American writer Patricia Raybon writes about how the oppression she felt in the United States had taught her to hate white people. She writes, "I hated them because they have lynched and lied and jailed and poisoned and neglected and discarded and excluded and exploited countless cultures and communities with such blatant intent or indifference as to humanly defy belief or understanding."[7] She goes on to say that she came to recognize that her hatred, no matter how legitimate and understandable, was eating away her identity and self-respect. It was blinding her to the gestures of friendship that a white girl in high school offered to her. She discovered that instead of waiting for whites to seek forgiveness for the injustices they had inflicted, she needed to ask for forgiveness for her own hatred, and for her inability to see a white person as a person and not just as part of a race of oppressors.

Hurt can be so painful that some victims create thick walls to protect themselves from more pain. However, if political liberation comes and those who were previously victims become the new masters, there is the danger that, still behind these thick walls, they will become in some ways like the old masters: defensive and aggressive at the same time.

Some of the oppressed, instead of acknowledging their hatred of the oppressor and their desire for revenge, get stuck in feelings of inferiority. Oppression has penetrated their own hearts. Convinced that they are inferior, they remain unable to react or to struggle for their rights.

They become their own oppressors.

In order to break the chain of violence and oppression that continues to rule in our world, oppressed people have to find liberation from these two attitudes: hatred towards others and hatred towards themselves. Only in this way, I believe, can the oppressed of the world find inner freedom and peace.

In 1996, when I visited Rwanda, a young woman told me that seventy-five members of her family had been massacred. "There is so much hate in my heart I do not know what to do with it," she said. "People are talking about reconciliation, but nobody has asked me to forgive them." Crimes of oppression and massacre leave deep wounds. Can they ever be healed? In order to be free, this woman needed help to accept her feelings of anger and revolt, reactions that made her feel guilty. But are these not natural, healthy reactions? It *is* important to express them. If this woman had not reacted, but had accepted passively the horror and injustices suffered by her people, wouldn't there be something wrong? Apathy in these circumstances would be a sign of depression and of a refusal to live. But this woman was able to say that she did not want revenge on those who had killed her family. She had seen enough killing.

Forgiveness is unilateral. It begins as the victim, with new-found strength, refuses to seek revenge, or, as in the case of the woman in prison, prays that the oppressor may change, refind truth, and admit his evil ways. Forgiveness is then to have hope for the oppressors, to believe in their humanity hidden under all their brokenness. It becomes reconciliation and a moment of communion of hearts if and when they seek forgiveness.

Liberating Ourselves from the Power of Hatred

A friend of mine wrote to me about her grandfather, an Australian who had served in the First World War. He had been gassed by the German army and was left permanently impaired. He remained terribly bitter towards all Germans. His bitterness poisoned his whole family and was passed down to the third generation, to my friend. In her letter she told me how she herself had absorbed her grandfather's attitudes and been influenced by the language he used to describe the German people: "Those wretched Huns!" he called them. It took a long time for this woman to learn to overcome her grandfather's legacy. It was a slow process to actively reject the attitudes inculcated in her at a young age. "All my life," she wrote, "I've tried to get rid of the prejudice against German people that has been programmed into me." Our hearts can be poisoned by words of hate and by the heritage of unresolved bitterness.

That is the reality of how human beings operate unless we choose forgiveness, both personally and as a community.

My friend continued in her letter, "I always think of that principle used by native North Americans, that in all important decisions, one must reflect on the consequences for the following generations . . . There must be millions and millions of us who carry the wounds of unforgiveness unto the third and fourth generations — or longer! The world carries this, and future wars or future peace depend on what we do with it."

Love of Enemies

The love of one's enemy is at the heart of the Christian message. Jesus says forcefully, "Love your enemies, do good to those who hate you, speak well of those who speak badly of you, and pray for those who abuse you" (Luke 6:27–28).

Jesus' words were spoken in Galilee, near Lake Tiberias. For many centuries the Jewish people had been overrun by foreign powers: first by the Babylonians, then by the Persians, later by the Greeks, and then by the Romans. The Jewish people, naturally, hated this foreign domination. Crushed in their dignity and freedom, they sought liberation, often through violent means. "Freedom fighters" might be the term the Jewish people would have used to describe those who resorted to violence. The Romans, of course, would have considered them terrorists.

Sometime after the birth of Christ, a certain Judas Ezechias led a powerful revolt in Galilee that was crushed by the Romans. Flavius Josephus, a Jewish historian of the first century, tells us that in retaliation for the revolt, the Romans crucified two thousand Galileans. And now Jesus is telling the Galileans to love their enemies! To pray for those who abuse and crush them! Imagine their anger! "No! I hate the Romans! I want to kill them!" you can hear them say. "They crucified my father, my brother, my son, my uncle. . . ." When we read Jesus' words in such a context an invitation to love our enemies might seem idealistic or even sentimental. For the Galileans, Jesus' words could seem like a provocation, the words of a coward, someone frightened of violence and confrontation. They might even think of Jesus as an agent of the Romans trying to dampen the true aspirations of the Jewish people for freedom.

But Jesus was neither provocative nor idealistic. He was making a promise of transformation and inner liberation that, if it had been received, could have transformed the history of the world.

The Dalai Lama points out the same truth in Buddhism:

> . . . the Bodhisattva affirms the importance of acquiring the right attitude towards your enemy. If you know how to develop a just attitude, your enemies become your spiritual masters, because their presence gives you an opportunity to grow in tolerance, patience, and understanding. As you acquire more patience and tolerance, it will be easier to develop your capacity for compassion, and thanks to that, your altruism.[8]

In the Koran, forgiveness of enemies is also important:

> It may be that Allah will grant love and friendship between you and those whom ye now hold as enemies. For Allah has power over all things; and Allah is oft-forgiving, most merciful.[9]

In order for humanity to break the chain of violence and hatred transmitted from generation to generation, to go from chaos to order, we have to take the words of Jesus, the Dalai Lama, and Muhammad seriously.

"Enemy" is a very strong word. It generally refers to those who are in a state of war. It can also be used to describe groups or individuals who oppress others, who shackle their freedom and prevent their growth. Because "enemy" is such a strong term, it's easy for us to deny that we have enemies. But when Christ, the Dalai Lama, and Muhammad all speak of enemies, they refer to something that can be much simpler, much closer to home. An enemy is someone who stands in the way of our freedom, dignity, and capacity to grow and to love, someone whom we avoid or with whom we refuse to communicate.

A woman spoke to me about her husband: "He is happy when I look after the house and children. He is happy when I cook good food and wash his clothes. He uses me sexually. But he never listens to me or treats me like a person, asking me for my opinion or advice. A lot of anger is coming up in me and I do not know what to do with it all." Her husband was becoming her enemy because he was crushing her dignity and her sense of self-worth. Dislike can grow to annoyance; annoyance can blossom into anger; anger can turn to hatred. We have to be careful not to let the seeds of our dislike grow and multiply. The words of Jesus and of other spiritual masters apply even to those mildest of negative feelings, our dislikes. To become truly free, to work for unity and peace, we have to work at all these relationships that cause us pain and dis-ease.

This woman's husband obviously needed to change. But didn't she need to change too? She had spent too much time obeying his whims and fancies; she had accepted being his servant just to please him. This woman had to discover and own her fears and flaws — all that led her to grant an unhealthy power to her husband. There is no question that both wife and husband needed help. For that woman, forgiving did not mean accepting a controlling, oppressive husband; it meant that she had to become more fully herself, standing up and affirming her own selfhood — with love, of course, and not out of anger — and then be ready to accept the consequences. To love one's enemy is not just a spiritual reality, but something essentially human.

All of us who think about peace, or even about the simple act of being human and of the process of growing towards maturity, must take this call to love our enemies seriously. This is a call to change, to no longer be controlled by our hurts and fears, but to enter instead into a truer relationship with those whom we dislike.

But to love those we dislike or even hate seems impossible. How can we love our enemies? Will they not just eat us up if we appear weak and vulnerable before them? How can we be open to someone who wants to curb our lives and our freedom? Life protects itself from death. If we see a stone hurtling towards us, don't we instinctively protect ourselves? How can we be open to someone who we think wants to hurt us physically or psychologically? Don't we need to protect ourselves when we are confronted by someone who, consciously or unconsciously, wants to prevent us, in some way, from blossoming forth and radiating life?

Awareness at the
Heart of Forgiveness

Forgiveness begins as we become aware of our fears and barriers. Patricia Raybon, who got over her hatred of all white people, and my Australian friend, who learned to overcome her hatred of all things German, could both start opening up to their "enemy" only when they realized how bitterness and anger were gripping them.

Hatred is like a gangrene: it eats a person up. All our refusals to communicate with others and to be open to them enclose us in a prison. But how do we move from accusation, no matter how legitimate it may be, to openness and acceptance, and even a desire to see our enemies liberated from their fears and selfishness? The process begins when we become aware of the walls within us that are built on fear and unconscious anger, and when we become aware of how our openness towards those we call friends can be a protection from anguish and loneliness.

This unveiling of our brokenness, fears, and faults does not come easily, precisely because it can enhance our feelings of worthlessness and lack of self-confidence. Instead of helping us to grow in love and forgiveness and openness, this process can close us up in subtle forms of depression and inertia. Where do we find the inner force that is stronger than our fears and barriers, that can liberate us from anger and dislikes and open us up to those who have hurt us?

I believe that the forces of life and the desires for communion are greater than the forces of death and hatred. At some moment in each of our lives there is an event that calls us to freedom and openness. At that point of epiphany we want to get out of the hole of depression and anger. We realize that we are imprisoned in ourselves or in our group, finding it difficult to relate to others.

A few years ago, Fred, a man in prison, wrote to me. He told me that he had committed a serious crime and had gone to jail. One day he became violent with other inmates and ended up in solitary confinement. Aware that he had lost everything — his family, his work, his mobility, as well as his dignity and self-respect — he wanted to die. But suddenly there rose up in him what he called "tiny stars of love," an urge to find himself and to rediscover love. It was a moment of grace. For many of us, it is only when we touch rock bottom, when all seems lost, that this tiny light of hope begins to shine. We become aware not only of all the darkness in ourselves, but also of the light of hope. At that moment an ascension begins.

To open up to others implies not only an awareness of our own fears, darkness, and brokenness, but also the presence of a light, a love, and an energy that will give us the desire to move forwards to openness and not let ourselves be controlled by the darkness.

The Desire to Be Liberated from Fear

The birth of this desire for liberation is a blessed moment, a moment of grace. It can happen when we meet those who are truly free and who sing their freedom. They reveal to us that freedom is possible and that it brings with it a blossoming of the heart in peace and joy. This desire for liberation may happen when we meet someone who loves and trusts us just as we are, and who sees, through our fears and inhibitions, all that is latent in us and can blossom forth with time. Love calls us forth and, like a magnet, attracts new and deep energies within.

This desire for liberation can come through dreams, through moments of inner quietness, or when we experience the presence of God loving us just as we are. In these "blessed moments," a consciousness of who we are rises up: we become aware of our importance, our blessedness, deeper than all the hurts that have governed our lives. For an instant we are no longer controlled by fear, anger, indifference, vengeance, or feelings of despair and unworthiness. A little light is born, a desire to be. Hope returns to our lives.

In the Bible, the prophet Ezekiel had a vision of a whole valley filled with dead bones. These bones represented the people of Israel who were saying, "Our bones are dry; we have no hope. All is over for us." Then, in the name of God, Ezekiel called them forth and spoke to them: "O my people, now I am going to open your graves. I will bring you up from your graves . . . I will put my Spirit in you and you will live" (Ezekiel 37:11–14). There are blessed moments when we feel called to rise up from the dirt and despair of our lives and to become fully alive.

Principles and Steps
Towards Forgiveness

I would suggest that there are three basic principles underlying forgiveness in the move towards reconciliation.

Principle 1: There can be no forgiveness of ourselves or of others unless we believe that we are all part of a common humanity. What this means in practical terms is that no one individual, no one group is superior to others. To say that we are all equally important seems a redundancy, and yet how often do any of us act as if it were true? How often has history demonstrated this human truth — that we are equal? Not often. So it needs to be said again and again. We may be different in race, culture, religion, and capacities, but we are all the same, with vulnerable hearts, the need to love and be loved, the needs to grow, to develop our capacities, and to find our place in the world. We all need to find ourselves of value. We are all the same because throughout our lives we have, every one of us, been hurt in one way or another. Fears have been implanted in us; we have difficulty relating to others; there is a certain chaos of anguish and violence within us.

In order to enter the path of forgiveness, we have to lose our feelings of both superiority and inferiority. Each of us has hurt another, each of us has been hurt. And so we must own and take responsibility for our lives as well as for the future. We are all called upon to stand up and take our place freely in the world.

Principle 2: To forgive means to believe that each of us can evolve and change, that human redemption *is* possible. We often lock people up in ready-made judgements: "He is a thief; she is disabled; he is schizophrenic." Perhaps this one did steal something, perhaps that one is disabled, but they are more than this. They are people who, if loved, helped, and trusted, can in some small way recognize their faults and their brokenness and can grow in humanity, in inner freedom, to do little acts of love.

Principle 3: To forgive means to yearn for unity and peace. Unity is the ultimate treasure. It is the place where, in the garden of humanity, each one of us can grow, bear fruit, and give life. That is what we all yearn for. When the father in the parable of the prodigal son sees his dishevelled son coming back to him thin, dirty, and un-shaven, he rushes out and kisses him. No judgement, no disagreeable remarks, not even "I forgive you." What the father yearned for was to be with his son again, to live a communion of hearts with him. His desire to be with his son was far greater than any hurts he may have suffered.

When someone loves deeply, forgiveness is evident. A lover wants to be with the loved one, that is all. If we love and want all people to be free to bear fruit, we will be a people of forgiveness. We will no longer be governed by our inner hurts or need to prove our worth; we will yearn for the growth of all people in peace and unity. To be a peacemaker and work for unity is a struggle. It is not easy to accept forgiveness or to forgive. It is not easy to shed our self-centredness. It is not easy to react against inertia or those feelings of fear that prevent us from entering into conflict.

At the heart of the process of forgiveness is the desire to be liberated from negative passions, from sharp dislikes and hatred. This is a desire that starts us on the road to true forgiveness. Having proposed three principles of forgiveness, let me now propose five steps.

The first step is the refusal to seek revenge. No more "an eye for an eye and a tooth for a tooth."

The second step is the genuine, heartfelt hope that the oppressor be liberated. The victim cannot change the heart that is filled with fear and hate, but one may hope and pray that one day the oppressor's heart of stone may become a heart of flesh.

The third step is the desire to understand the oppressors: how and why their indifference or hardness of heart has developed, and how they might be liberated.

The fourth step is the recognition of our own darkness. We, too, have hurt people and perhaps have contributed to the hardness of the oppressors.

The fifth step is patience. It takes time for a victim to be freed from blockage and hatred; it takes time for an oppressor to evolve and to change.

Changing the Heart of the Oppressors

Reconciliation is a bilateral affair; it is the completion of the forgiveness process, the coming together of the oppressed and the oppressor, each one accepting the other, each acknowledging their fears and hatreds, each accepting that the path of mutual love is the only way out of a world of conflict.

It is difficult, however, for the oppressor to admit guilt. Let us try to understand why. It might help us both to exercise authority with greater sensitivity and to walk the road of forgiveness.

Power has a direction: it is always exercised downwards,

towards the weak. One manifestation of power in the family, for example, is the authority of parents over their children. But power is quickly equated with what is right. Don't most parents feel that they know what is best for their children? Don't all those in positions of power think they know what is right and seem incapable of accepting any kind of criticism? The exercise of power gives people a sense of identity and worth.

Those in authority who doubt or waver in their decisions do not inspire confidence. In many ways, the mighty feel that they are in the image of the Almighty, that they should not be questioned, only obeyed. Yet we are all broken, turned in on ourselves, self-centred, needing success, power, and recognition. So few of us have the necessary maturity and wisdom to exercise authority in a loving and freeing way through what we might call "servant leadership," helping people to find trust in themselves and to grow in freedom.

It is difficult for those with power to allow themselves to be governed by the superior law of love. It is equally difficult for them to admit that they have hurt those who are weaker. We all have the capacity to push all the wrongs we have committed into the secret recesses of our being. We develop sophisticated techniques to silence the conscience and erase every trace of remorse. Psychologists have described this ability to render ourselves numb; Freud called it a "protective shield" that we create around threatening feelings.

Geiko Müller-Fahrenholz, a German theologian who has worked with the World Council of Churches, wrote a remarkable book called *The Art of Forgiveness*. In it he says that people generally manage to forget the wrongs they have done. "There can be no forgiveness," he says, "where perpetrators, whether individuals or collective, lack the courage to disarm themselves in front of the victims. This is a painful and demanding act."[10]

When those who have created a sense of self-worth and personal identity through the exercise of power finally reveal their wrongs, forswear the evil in themselves, and ask their victims for forgiveness, then they renounce the supremacy that power presumes and accept the loss of their self-esteem. It is as if they have become naked and vulnerable. As they break through the protective shield that gave them a false sense of self-worth, anguish and a feeling of inner death can arise. But, at the same time, they are liberated from guilt and develop a new, deeper sense of self-worth. That is why the emotions can be so great when oppressor and oppressed are reconciled.

It is difficult to exercise authority always with wisdom and with a desire to serve. I know I sometimes stifled others in the community of l'Arche when I was the leader. It is difficult to admit our faults and the wrongs we may have done. It is even more difficult when these wrongs are serious and we have severely wounded others.

It is also difficult for those who trust their leaders to believe that they might have done wrong. Many of us are programed to obey and not to question or criticize. There is a real growth in us when we recognize such wrongs and take action to correct them.

The Gentle Power of God

For true reconciliation, in most cases we need a force that transcends both the oppressed and oppressor. Geiko Müller-Fahrenholz writes:

> In the last resort, humans cannot define what constitutes their humanity. It transcends them. As we work for forgiveness, we are called to reflect that as human beings, each of us is created in the image of God, the most Merciful. This is our calling, our mission: to become mirrors of mercy.[11]

We all tend to wear masks, the mask of superiority or of inferiority, the mask of worthiness or of victim. It is not easy to let our masks come off and to discover the little child inside us who yearns for love and for light, and who fears being hurt. Forgiveness, however, implies the removal of these masks, an acceptance of who we really are: that we have been hurt, and that we have hurt others.

Forgiveness of ourselves, then, implies an acceptance of our true value. The loss of a false self-image, if it is an image of superiority, or the need to hide our brokenness can bring anguish and inner pain. We can only accept this pain if we discover our true self beneath all the masks and realize that if we are broken, we are also more beautiful than we ever dared to suspect. When we realize our brokenness, we do not have to fall into depression; when we see our true beauty, we do not have to become proud as peacocks. Seeing our own brokenness and beauty allows us to recognize, hidden under the brokenness and self-centredness of others, their beauty, their value, and their sacredness. This discovery is sometimes a leap in the dark, a blessed moment, a moment of grace, and a moment of enlightenment that comes in a meeting with the God of Love, who reveals to us that we are beloved and so is everyone else.

As the desire grows in us to be whole and to struggle for this wholeness in ourselves, in others, in our community, and in the world, and as we desire to be free in order to free others, a new energy is born within us, an energy that flows from God. It is as though we are crossing the Red Sea from slavery to freedom. We can start to live the pain of loss and accept anguish because a new love and a new consciousness of self are being given to us.

Jesus' invitation to love one's enemies must have appeared dangerously utopian to the Galileans. Maybe it was only when they saw him standing up to the religious leaders of his day, pursuing a courageous and dangerous course for love, truth, and the liberation of the oppressed, that some began to understand that this was a new way to struggle for peace and to break the seemingly unending chain of human oppression. Loving our enemies means to see them as individuals who are perhaps caught up in a cycle of fear, and of oppression, and in their character traits and need for power, but who are individuals nonetheless and are, beneath everything, sacred and precious. Their secret person is hidden behind walls of fear. To love them is to hope and yearn that instead of living a form of self-destruction, locked up in their own pride and power, they can be liberated.

If, the night before he died, Jesus knelt down humbly before his disciples, washed their feet, and called them to do the same, was it not because he knew how power can be used to crush and enslave, rather than to empower and free? In order to empower and free others, we need to discover this new force of love and communion, which comes from God.

This vision of love seems humanly impossible. One day in 1944, in the Auschwitz concentration camp, a group of men stood waiting to be executed. Suddenly, a man stepped forward and volunteered to replace one of the men who had been condemned to death. He was Father Maximilian Kolbe. The commandant was startled, but he allowed the priest to take the man's place. So Father Kolbe joined the group of men in the bunker, where he helped each one to make the final passage of death. When all had died and he was alone the guards came and killed him too. By doing this, Father Kolbe was bearing witness that love is stronger than death.

More recently, in 1996 in Algeria, the trappist monk Christian de Chergé was murdered along with six of his brother monks. They had refused to leave their monastery in a dangerous and unprotected area in order to bear witness to the presence of God, who loves every human being whatever their religion. Christian left a document with his mother to be opened when he died. In it he gives thanks:

> In this "thank you," which is said for everything in my life, I certainly include you, friends of yesterday and

today . . . and you also, friend of my final moment, who would not be aware of what you were doing. Yes, for you too, I want to say this "thank you" and *à Dieu* [to God], whom I have seen through you. May we meet again in Paradise as two blessed and good thieves, if that is what God, the Father of us both, wants. Amen! Inch'Allah![12]

There we have the supreme gift, the gift of forgiveness!

Jesus' invitation to love our enemies is also a promise, true for Christians and non-Christians alike: what we cannot do by ourselves, we can do with this inner power of the Spirit, which transforms our hearts of stone, founded on fear, into hearts of flesh, open and vulnerable to others. Through the gift of the Spirit of God we receive a new power that permits us to stand firm in love.

We Work and God Works

Forgiveness, the act of loving my enemy, like forgiveness of self, is not a sudden event, a rapid change of heart. Most of the time it is a long process that begins with the desire to be free, to accept ourselves as we are, and to grow in the love of those who are different and those who have hurt us or appear as rivals. It is the process of getting out of the prison of our likes and dislikes, our hatreds and fears, and walking to freedom and compassion. In the process of liberation, there may still be inhibitions, resentments, and anger, but there is also this growing desire to be free.

I believe that this desire comes from God, who lives deep within each of us, but it must be coupled with our own efforts, for example, to stop rejoicing when people talk badly of our enemies, to stop criticizing and belittling others, and to hold onto our poison-spreading tongues. It might mean befriending those who befriend our enemy, so that we might begin to understand our enemy. It also means struggling against feeling like victims and so hiding behind fear, depression, anger, and inertia.

To understand the enemy both within us and outside of us is an important part of forgiveness. If we work at it, God works in us, and, one day, resentments start to disappear. Forgiveness is to begin to love and to accept ourselves, trying to understand and appreciate all that is valuable in us all, praying that what blocks us all from being free may break like a dam, so that what is most precious in us may flow forth. That is the final prayer of Jesus: "Father, forgive them, for they know not what they do" (Luke 23:34).

To forgive is to break down the walls of hostility that separate us, and to bring each other out of the anguish of loneliness, fear, and chaos into communion and oneness. This communion is born from mutual trust and acceptance, and the freedom to be ourselves in our uniqueness and beauty, the freedom to exercise our gifts. We are no longer contained and held back by fear, prejudices, or the need to prove ourselves.

So the sense of belonging that is necessary for the opening of our hearts is born when we walk together, needing each other, accompanying one another whether we are weak or strong, capable or not. This belonging will not bring feelings of superiority if we are walking towards inner freedom. It will not seek to exclude but to include the weak, the needy, and the different, for they have a secret power that opens up people's hearts and leads them to compassion and mutual trust. This belonging becomes a song of gratitude for each one of us.

Of course, all this takes time. But are we not all called to take this journey if we want to become fully human, to conquer divisions and oppression, and to work for peace? If each one of us today begins this journey and has the courage to forgive and be forgiven, we will no longer be governed by past hurts. Wherever we may be — in our families, our work places, with friends, or in places of worship or of leisure — we can rise up and become agents of a new land. But let us not put our sights too high. We do not have to be saviours of the world! We are simply human beings, enfolded in weakness and in hope, called together to change our world one heart at a time.

NOTES

Quotations from the Bible in this work are from the Revised Standard Version, or are Jean Vanier's direct translations from the Greek.

1. Martin Buber, *Le Chemin de l'homme* (Paris: Éditions du Rocher, 1989) 19. Used by permission.

2. Henri J.M. Nouwen, *Adam, God's Beloved* (Maryknoll, NY: Orbis, 1997) 101. Copyright © 1997 by the Estate of Henri J.M. Nouwen. Used by permission.

3. Aung San Suu Kyi, Nobel Peace Prize acceptance speech.

4. Rudyard Kipling, *Poems of Rudyard Kipling* (New York: Gramercy, 1995).

5. Nelson Mandela, *Long Walk to Freedom* (New York: Little, Brown, 1994) 544. Copyright © 1994 Nelson Rolihlahla Mandela. Used by permission of Little, Brown and Company.

6. Donald Nicholl, *The Beatitude of Truth: Reflections of a Lifetime*. Ed. Adrien Hastings. (London: Darton Longman and Todd, 1997) 160–61. Used by permission.

7. Patricia Raybon, *My First White Friend: Confessions on Race, Love, and Forgiveness* (New York: Viking Press, 1996) 4. Copyright © 1996 by Patricia Raybon. Used by permission of Viking Penguin, a division of Penguin Putnam Inc.

8. Dalai Lama, *Le Dalai-Lama Parle de Jésus* (Paris: Éditions Brepols) 44–45.

9. Surah 60:7, New Revised Edition.

10. Geiko Müller-Fahrenholz, *The Art of Forgiveness: Theological Reflections on Healing and Reconciliation* (Geneva: WCC Publications, 1997) 26. Used by permission.

11. Müller-Fahrenholz, XI.

12. Christian de Chergé, "Testament," *The Tablet* 8 June 1996.